kamera
BOOKS

www.kamerabooks.com

Brian Mills

101 FORGOTTEN FILMS

kamera
BOOKS

First published in 2008 by Kamera Books
PO Box 394, Harpenden, Herts, AL5 1XJ
www.kamerabooks.com

A CIP catalogue record for this book is available from the British Library.

ISBN-13: 978-1-84243-252-5

Book typeset by Elsa Mathern
Printed and bound in Great Britain by Cox & Wyman, Reading

CONTENTS

INTRODUCTION

Somewhere in the labyrinth of our memories are films that we have seen and cannot forget but frustratingly may never see again because they have mysteriously vanished from the public domain. They may be hidden away in a film studio's vault, buried beneath the floorboards of a filmmaker's home, imprisoned by some ancient legality, refused release at a director's whim, or simply not optioned by a distributor. This book attempts to exhume some of the films that are entombed in a cinema cemetery and in so doing unearth a film noir masterpiece, a French classic, a Mastroianni feature comparable to *Cinema Paradiso*, a Joan Crawford headliner, and an Edward G Robinson comedy. There are lost films of Ernst Lubitsch, John Ford, Alfred Hitchcock, Elia Kazan, Sergio Leone, Nicholas Ray, Bo Widerberg, Roberto Benigni and Robert Altman.

In researching these films, I was saddened to see how many there were from the 1950s, a period when I was a cinema projectionist working at the Gaumont cinema in the East End of London. The mid-50s were Hollywood's halcyon days and I was a star-struck kid who had fallen head-over-heels in love with the movies. As I re-run these screen gems in my head I have tried to project to you the passion that I felt when I saw them: *Six Bridges To Cross*, *The Great Man*, *A Hatful of Rain*, *A Man is Ten Feet Tall*, *Wind Across the Everglades* and *Middle of the Night*.

It is my sincere wish that the 101 films in this book will some day be re-released and while compiling this list it was comforting to know that I had to remove a few titles because they have since been distributed on DVD: *Mon Ange*, *A Woman in Winter*, *Illusion* and *The Other Side of the Wind*, the latter named being the unfinished last film of Orson Welles that will be completed by Peter Bogdanovich and theatrically distributed worldwide in 2008.

PRECIOUS GEMS

Among films that have disappeared are some that have defied conventional cinema and become cult classics, pushing the boundaries beyond normality. It may be that they have shown an actor in a different light, used narration in a new way, employed a way of storytelling that makes one question what one is being presented with, celebrated the magical visionary art of cinema through film, or examined the dictates of the star system and its effect upon us.

Letty Lynton   1932

Directed by: Clarence Brown
Written by: John Meehan. Marie Belloc Lowndes (novel).
Cast: Joan Crawford (Letty Lynton), Robert Montgomery (Hale Darrow), Nils Asther (Emile Renaul), Lewis Stone (District Attorney Haney), May Robson (Mrs Lynton), Louise Closser Hale (Miranda), Emma Dunn (Mrs Darrow), Walter Walker (Mr Darrow), William Pawley (Hennessey).

Story: Letty Lynton (Crawford) is a New York socialite who is disgusted with her philandering ways and in particular with her Latin lover Emile Renaul (Asther). She sails for New York and onboard meets a wealthy businessman Hale Darrow (Montgomery). They fall in love. 'I'd black your boots for the rest of my life!' she tells him, but he doesn't know of her past and she doesn't know that Emile is following her. There is a poignant scene, which captures Letty's loneliness: all passengers receive Christmas telegrams from loved ones at home, except Letty.

Jerry, seeing her sadness, pretends that he didn't get one either. Arriving in New York they are swamped by the press, eager to report their engagement, but Emile is among the crowd, hoping to rekindle Letty's love for him and take her back to South America. She manages to avoid any confrontation with Emile, but he turns up at her mother's house and threatens to show her love letters to him to the press and to Jerry if she doesn't agree to see him at his hotel that evening. An argument ensues at the hotel resulting in Emile accidentally drinking a poisoned drink intended for Letty.

What the millions who have not seen this film are sadly missing is the remarkable performance by Joan Crawford. The scene where she betrays her true feelings of hatred toward Emile are seen first in close up as she listens to him singing in the next room: guilt, anger, loathing, fear and confusion are all expressed in that one moment. Letty's verbal outburst follows like a volcanic eruption as she stares at her dying lover, each uttered word falling on her victim like molten lava. 'Yes, I did it! I meant it for myself… I'm glad I did it! You dirty, filthy, greedy mongrel! I'm glad I did it! If I hang for it, I'm glad I did it!'

RARITY VALUE: 5/5

Theatrically released in 1932, *Letty Lynton* caused a nationwide fashion craze for the ruffled-shoulder organdie dress worn by Crawford, which sold 50,000 copies at Macy's New York store alone. The film is a showcase for designer Adrian's dresses. In January 1936 a court decision ruled that MGM violated copyright laws by too closely following the script of Edward Sheldon's play *Dishonoured Lady*, which was based on a girl named Madeleine Smith who lived in Glasgow and was brought to trial upon an indictment for twice attempting to poison her lover, and then for actually poisoning him. She was acquitted. MGM claimed unsuccessfully that they had based their screenplay on the novel *Letty Lynton* by Marie Belloc Lowndes.

The film was banned in England on grounds that it 'justified homicide without penalty'. In the film, Letty is saved from execution by an alibi from a man who claims she spent the night in question with him.

Due to the 1936 court ruling against MGM, public exhibition or show-ing of the film on television is strictly prohibited. Only poor bootleg copies remain that do nothing to enhance the film.

Joan Crawford: Born Lucille LeSueur in San Antonio, Texas, in 1908. Debuted in *Miss MGM* in 1925. Won an Oscar for *Mildred Pierce*. Wanting to be a dancer since she was a child, despite an accident that severely injured her foot, she persisted in pursuing her dream and eventually entered a dance contest and won. She said: 'I knew I was born with talent, though I didn't know exactly what it was.' She learned every dance step she could. She went to Chicago and got a job doing a song and dance act in an out-of-town café. Two weeks later and Joan was in the chorus line at a club in Detroit. She subsequently appeared in the revue *Innocent Eyes* in New York and then in *The Passing Show* of 1924. Eight months later and she was spotted by a talent scout and asked to do a screen test for MGM. She started working for MGM thinking that they had employed her for her dancing, but they wanted her as an actress. Her first screen part was as a chorus girl covered in snow in *Pretty Ladies*. MGM wanted to change her name and held a competition in the magazine *Photoplay* to get the name that was, of course, Joan Crawford, a name which she always hated, saying that it sounded like 'Crowfish'. But it was important to Joan to make a name for herself as a film star to prove to her friends and family back home, who didn't believe in her, that she had talent. In 1928 she played in *Our Dancing Daughters* and had a lucky break when she was seen coming out of a cake and dancing on a table. Suddenly she was a star and was given a raise of 500 dollars a week. Joan wanted to be a real actress and would hang around the set watching Greta Garbo work whenever she could. She finally pestered Louis B Mayer for more dra-matic roles. She was with MGM for 17 years. During those years she became one of the ten top movie stars. But it was at Warner Broth-ers that she gained the dramatic role that would win her an Academy Award. The film was *Mildred Pierce* and it told of a housewife who becomes a successful businesswoman only to find herself suspected of murdering her second husband. Joan was also Oscar nominated for Best Actress for her roles in *Possessed* and *Sudden Fear*.

Larceny Inc.   1942

Directed by: Lloyd Bacon
Written by: Laura Perelman. SJ Perelman.
Cast: Edward G Robinson (J Chalmers 'Pressure' Maxwell), Jane Wyman (Denny Costello), Broderick Crawford (Jug Martin), Jack Carson (Jeff Randolph), Anthony Quinn (Leo Dexter), Edward Brophy (Weepy Davis), Harry Davenport (Homer Bigelow), John Qualen (Sam Bacharach), Barbara Jo Allen (Mademoiselle Gloria), Grant Mitchell (Mr Aspinwall), Jackie Gleason (Hobart), Andrew Tombes (Oscar Englehart), Joe Downing (Smitty), George Meeker (Mr Jackson), Fortunio Bonanova (Anton Copoulos).

Story: Released from prison, Pressure Maxwell (Robinson) and Jug Martin (Crawford) are greeted by Denny Costello (Wyman). Pressure promises Denny that he will go straight, but when he has a bank loan turned down to open a dog track, he resorts to trusted methods to get the money. He gets a sidekick Weepy (Edward Brophy) to case the cellar of a luggage store next door to a bank. Buying the store from its owner, Pressure sets about getting stock from luggage salesman Jeff Randolph (Jack Carson) and then immediately gets Jug to start drilling in the basement. Meanwhile the store has to keep open to give the impression that business is as normal. Pressure has no idea of selling etiquette and prices everything the same, taking umbrage when customers expect purchased goods to be wrapped. Chaos continues when Jug drills through a water pipe. A contingency of neighbours led by Sam Bacharach (John Qualen) asks Pressure to get the contractor to repair the street. Denny learns that Jug is digging into the bank and complains to Pressure. Once the street is fixed, the store is closed for alterations. Aspinwall (Grant Mitchell), the banker, offers to buy the store for $12,000, but Pressure wants more. Jug thinks he has hit oil but it is only a fuel tank. They catch a man, Smitty (Joe Downing), attempting to rob their store and Pressure in desperation gives him a bag. Neighbours bring gifts to Pressure, while, in prison, Smitty tells Leo (Anthony Quinn) about the bank job. At the re-opening they make $535 profit in one day. Pressure tells Denny that he likes the honest business, but then Leo comes in and orders them to rob the bank. And from then on things only get worse and consequently even funnier.

The screenplay is based on the stage play *Night Before Christmas* written by Laura and SJ Perelman and a lot of the craziness of Perelman's lines remain in the film. He was one of Hollywood's funniest writers and of course wrote the Marx Brothers' comedies, *Monkey Business* and *Horse Feathers*, as well as one of Hollywood's most brilliant romantic comedies *One Night With Venus*. Edward G Robinson excels as Pressure Maxwell, managing to portray his typecast gangster self in a hilarious scenario. His anti-salesmanlike behaviour is a joy to behold and is side-bustingly funny.

RARITY VALUE: 4/5
Can sometimes be seen on television channels but still unreleased on DVD or VHS.

Edward G Robinson: Born Emanuel Goldenberg on 12 December 1893 in Bucharest, Romania. He arrived in the USA at the age of ten, when his parents moved into New York's East Side. He attended City College with plans to become either a rabbi or a lawyer, but abandoned both aspirations to become an actor. He was awarded a scholarship at the American Academy of Dramatic Arts and began to work in stock under his new name of Robinson. Later came Broadway and then his film debut in the silent film *The Bright Shawl* in 1923. But it was the advent of sound that really gave him his breakthrough and allowed his voice to reverberate in our memories with the character of gangster Rico Bandello in 1931's *Little Caesar*. Other memorable roles followed including that of insurance investigator Keyes in Wilder's classic film noir *Double Indemnity* in 1944, which made use of a now-famous plot device: throughout the film, Fred MacMurray's character Walter Neff is constantly lighting Keyes' cigars for him; at the end, as he is dying, Keyes returns the favour, lighting Neff's cigarette. 'You know why you couldn't figure this one out Keyes? I was too close to you, right across the desk from you.' 'Closer than that,' replies Keyes. It is spoken in this rich familiar voice that so many have impersonated, a voice that Robinson cultivated by his habitual smoking of cigars. He had a passion for collecting things, whether cigar bands or art paintings, and this reflected an actor who was a connoisseur of life.

See: *Sammy Going South.*

Appointment With Danger   1951

Directed by: Lewis Allen
Written by: Richard L Breen. Warren Duff.
Cast: Alan Ladd (Al Goddard), Phyllis Calvert (Sister Augustine), Paul Stewart (Earl Boettiger), Jan Sterling (Dodie), Jack Webb (Joe Regas), Stacey Harris (Paul Ferrer), Harry Morgan (George Soderquist), David Wolfe (David Goodman), Dan Riss (Maury Ahearn), Geraldine Wall (Mother Ambrose), George J Lewis (Leo Cronin), Paul Lees (Gene Gunner).

Story: Al Goddard (Ladd) is a special investigator for the US post office who is called in to investigate the murder of a postal inspector. He questions the only witness to the crime, a nun, Sister Augustine (Calvert). She has seen two men drag a body onto a street and is able to recognise one of the men from a mugshot. Goddard hears that the motive for the killing has to do with a planned one-million-dollar mail truck robbery, which will involve three hoodlums and the mail truck driver. Managing to infiltrate the gang by bribery, he schemes to foil the criminals. Discovering Goddard's true identity, the gang take him and the nun prisoners, which leads to a climactic shoot-out in a dismal industrial district.

At first viewing this seems like a mediocre film noir but on closer inspection it is disturbingly gripping, which is mainly due to casting Jack

Webb as one of the villains. Webb, who was later to gain fame as Joe Friday in the successful TV series *Dragnet*, is viciously and convincingly vile. His partner in *Dragnet*, Harry Morgan, is his accomplice in *Appointment With Danger*. There is a telling sequence when Goddard is playing Joe Regas (Webb) at squash and uses the ball as a weapon to floor him.

RARITY RATING: 4/5
Some bootleg DVD copies of questionable quality can be obtained via the Internet.

Alan Ladd: Laddie, as he was nicknamed, appeared in 95 films from *Tom Brown of Culver* in 1932 to *The Carpetbaggers* in 1964. He won a Golden Globe Award in 1954 for World Favourite Male Actor. Rose immediately to stardom when he was cast to play Philip Raven, a professional killer in *This Gun For Hire*. He set the pattern for the smooth-talking, handsome killer with a sartorial sense of elegance. Seven movies were made teaming him with Veronica Lake, a screen partnership that worked successfully in *The Glass Key* and *The Blue Dahlia*. But it was in 1953 that Laddie got the role that epitomised him as the hero in George Stevens' archetypal western *Shane*. The film was based on Jack Schaefer's novel and told the story of a retired gunslinger, Shane, who drifts into a homestead where the family is being terrorised by a cattleman and his hired gun. In motion picture history *Shane* earned itself the critical laurel of being one of the greatest westerns of all time. The voice of an actor is paramount to his success and Laddie had the most distinctive voice of them all, as witnessed in an early bit part in the film *Citizen Kane* when he played a reporter whose voice can be heard from out of a group of shadowy figures. Despite his success, Laddie never believed the hype of the media or even his fans, and until the day he died maintained that he had the face of an ageing choirboy and the build of an undernourished featherweight.

See: *The Great Gatsby.*

Blast of Silence

Directed by: Allen Baron
Written by: Allen Baron. Waldo Salt (wrote narration).
Cast: Allen Baron (Frankie Bono), Molly McCarthy (Lorrie), Larry Tucker (Big Ralph), Peter Clume (Troiano), Danny Meehan (Peter), Dean Sheldon (Nightclub Singer), Charles Creasap (Contact Man), Bill DePrato (Sailor), Erich Kollmar (Bellhop).

Story: Frankie 'Baby Boy' Bono, born into pain. Frankie Bono, out of Cleveland and into murder. Frankie is a loner but he likes it that way. He is a professional killer with hatred in his heart, a gun in his pocket and a contract to eliminate a Manhattan mobster named Troiano. He needs a gun with a silencer and calls on Big Ralph to supply it but it will take a day to get it so he has time to kill and that he can do – it is Christmas and he remembers other Christmases, at the orphanage, always wishing for something. Suddenly he meets an old friend and his sister, Lorrie, a girl he once loved, and is persuaded to attend their Christmas party. For a moment he forgets who he is and begins to enjoy himself, dancing with Lorrie and even accepting the challenge of a peanut-pushing-with-your-nose contest, which he wins. Next day he accepts Lorrie's invitation for dinner and then suddenly he gets angry when she starts asking too many questions. Everything seems to go wrong and Lorrie asks him to leave. December 26, another day. Troiano is back and so is Frankie, shadowing him as he watches him enter a brownstone building to meet a woman. He is beginning to hate Troiano as much as he hated his old man. He follows him to a nightclub called The Village Gate and is surprised to see Big Ralph there too. When Ralph realises whom Frankie is planning to hit, he wants more money. Ralph is now a problem and Frankie follows him home and kills him. The man who has hired Frankie to kill Troiano is not interested in his excuses for killing Ralph and when Frankie tells him that he no longer wants to do the job, he is told that he is in serious trouble. Next day Frankie meets another contact, a guy named Bonaface, and picks up the gun. He waits for Troiano to leave his apartment before he checks it out. The time is getting closer for the killing. It will be his last one. One more to die and then he will be alone. He gets to thinking about Lorrie, her voice reverberating in his head, 'What you need is a girl so that you don't have to be alone'. Frankie visits her again. It is early and she is surprised to see him. He tells her that she is right; he needs a girl. 'What I'm saying is that I need you.' But Lorrie isn't alone; her boyfriend appears from the bathroom. Frankie has got it all wrong… again. Angrily he leaves. Focus, he must focus. A killer who doesn't kill, gets killed. When Troiano returns to his apartment, Frankie is waiting for him, five shots and he's dead. Job done. Exit via the fire escape and then just one more contact to pick up the money. He is taken out to a pier. It is blowing a hurricane. Bad moment. There are hoodlums waiting for him, another bad moment. Frankie realises that he is the payoff. There is nowhere to run, nowhere to hide. Gunshots. Pain. Falling into an abyss. Out of Cleveland into death. Alone. Silence.

One of the finest film noirs ever made. It captures all the qualities and nuances of the genre: ominous shadows, jazzy soundtrack, bleak landscapes, a central character who is a loner and unhappy, and dealing with death every day, often his own. There is always a girl, too, that he struggles to win but invariably loses due to bad luck or unrequited love. *Blast of Silence* has all the aforementioned in abundance despite being made on a low budget, its handheld camera movements adding to the edginess and tenseness that we feel in watching a professional killer at work. For the first time the audience is allowed into the consciousness of a killer by using narration throughout the movie, the rich gravel tones of Lionel Stander, prodding Frankie Bono ceaselessly, like picking at a scab. Baron's acting debut as Bono is as mesmerising as Gazzara's was in *End as a Man* (aka *The Strange One*). His loneliness and incongruity are never more emphasised than in the Christmas party sequence where he sits on his own like a cactus on a couch, all prickly and dry, observing a world so alien to him that it could be on another planet. When the late Alexander Walker, film critic of London's *Evening Standard*, reviewed *Blast of Silence* on its West End release in 1961, he called Baron the 'new Orson Welles' and there are definitely Wellesian touches in the film, like when a camera is positioned on the sidewalk, its low angle waiting for the distant figure of Bono to walk towards it while a jazz score heightens its pitch. But if Baron can be likened to any director, it would be Cassavetes, who, like him, broke the motion-picture mould and altered the way we look at movies. Allen Baron was a master maverick and *Blast of Silence* was a piece of the master.

RARITY RATING: 4/5

Occasionally shown theatrically at art house retrospectives, most recently in France. DVD bootleg copies appear on Ebay of various qualities, otherwise not available on video. Original print is held in the vaults of Universal Studios.

Allen Baron: Baron's flirtation with cinema has been short but memorable: directing and acting in only two feature films. Most of his career, which saw him starting out in 1959 as assistant director and actor in *Cuban Rebel Girl*, has been directing TV series: *Hawaiian Eye* in the early 1950s to *Fortune Dane* in the mid-1980s. Sandwiched between these were episodes that he directed for many successful shows from *The Brady Bunch* to *Charlie's Angels*. But one can only speculate what might have been had Baron concentrated his talents on the bigger screen. *Blast of Silence* is a masterpiece but is only now being recognised as such. It is almost as if he created his own film noir image of himself and is now stepping out of the shadow that it projected. One feels that a lot more will be revealed by the man himself with the release of the documentary *Requiem for a Killer: The Making of 'Blast of Silence'*. Perhaps someone will buy his unsold dramatic pilot for NBC called *Two Young Men and a Girl in a Meat Grinder* and share it with us cinephiles. We may even get to see the screenplay that was turned into a feature called *Deadly Love*. We may.

See: *Terror in the City*.

Splendor   1989

Directed by: Ettore Scola
Written by: Ettore Scola
Cast: Marcello Mastroianni (Jordan), Massimo Troisi (Luigi), Marina Vlady (Chantal), Paolo Panelli (Paolo), Pamela Villoresi (Eugenia), Giacomo Piperno (Lo Fazio).

Story: Jordan (Mastroianni) is the ageing manager of Splendor, a cinema that is gradually losing out to television in the popularity stakes and threatened by closure to make way for a department store. As Jordan sits in the stalls, he reflects on Splendor's glory days when it was so popular that police had to be called to stop the waiting crowds from rioting. He remembers the excitement that he felt when his father took his travelling cinema through towns showing Lang's *Metropolis*. By the time that Jordan had graduated to manager of Splendor, the cinema was the focus of entertainment for the townspeople and each film played to packed houses. He had fallen in love with a chorus girl Chantal (Vlady) and persuaded her to become an usherette at his cinema, but their love was never consummated and another admirer, Luigi (Troisi), followed her into Splendor and became its projectionist.

Jordan struggles to clear the mounting debts partially caused by poor attendance at directors' retrospectives. Jordan's life is and always will be film, and he is determined to reignite Splendor's patrons with their forgotten passion for pictures. There is a wonderful Capraesque sequence where he imagines friends gathering around him to stop him from selling. Appropriately, the film ends with a further homage to Capra with the climactic scene from *It's a Wonderful Life*.

Splendor is a cinematic gem for film lovers and unashamedly celebrates the greatest entertainment in the world. It can be likened to *Cinema Paradiso* and *Dopo Mezzanotte* in that it blows cinema a kiss. Film buffs will relish the chance of recognising some classic film clips, particularly from Italian cinema. The three leading actors are faultless and I don't think Mastroianni has ever been better. Why this film has not been released on DVD beggars belief.

RARITY RATING: 5/5

The only chance of seeing this film is by pestering your art house cinema manager or writing to Warner Brothers who seem to own the Italian rights to it.

Marcello Mastroianni: Films were the sweet life for Mastroianni. 'They come for you in the morning in a limousine; they take you to the studio; they stick a pretty girl in your arms. They call that a profession? Come on!' He crammed in as many films as he could during his life, 143 to be exact, from an uncredited appearance in *Marionette* in 1939 to his final performance in *Journey to the Beginning of the World* in 1997. Fondly remembered for his leading roles as the playboy in *La Dolce Vita* and as the filmmaker in *8½*, both made for Federico Fellini, Mastroianni epitomised the passionate and enigmatic Italian. He even put on dancing shoes in the screen's homage to Astaire and Rogers in *Ginger and Fred*. Snaporaz, as Fellini called him, was born in Fontana Lisi in 1924. During World War Two he was sent to a German concentration camp, but managed to escape to Venice. He began work for Eagle Lion Films in Rome and joined a drama club before being discovered by director Luchino Visconti, who later featured him in his film *Le Notti Bianche*. *Making a Film for Me Is to Live* was the title of a documentary that he made for TV in 1996 and his sentiments were echoed when he said, 'In front of the camera, I feel solid, satisfied.'

And even the end of his life, reportedly dying in the arms of his real-life love Catherine Deneuve, must have seemed like the perfect fade-out for the man who loved movies.

Giorgino   1994

Directed by: Laurent Boutonnat
Written by: Laurent Boutonnat. Gilles Laurent.
Cast: Jeff Dahlgren (Giorgio/Giorgino), Mylene Farmer (Catherine), Joss Ackland (Father Glaise), Louise Fletcher (Innkeeper), Frances Barber (Marie).

Story: A child's face in close up, shyly smiling. A nun approaches and calls him Valli. Another voice, a man's, says that he is Valli. The man looks weary and ill, and is taken in to be examined by a doctor. His stethoscope prods the man's chest and the doctor hears wheezing. 'Mustard gas,' he proclaims. 'You are lucky to be alive,' he tells him. 'You have enough lung left to breathe awhile.' Giorgino Valli, a French lieutenant home from the war, is searching for the retarded children that he once looked after; some call them mad, he calls them different. When he returns to the institution they have gone. The caretaker gives him a pile of returned letters that he wrote to the children. A horse is about to be slaughtered outside their window, but Valli buys it for 600 francs. He offers the lady a stick of candy. 'The war hurt you bad, didn't it?' she says to him. Valli journeys through the snow to Dr Grace's Orphanage. There, he is asked to save the life of Madam Grace, who has tried to hang herself rather than face the agonies of diphtheria, but he fails. As he leaves her room he sees a beautiful woman and enquires whom she is and is told that she is Catherine, Dr Grace's daughter. Once again he asks about the children and is told that they died long ago. Desperately he searches the dormitories and finds them empty but for a few dolls. But he doesn't stop searching, always asking, 'What happened to the children?' His question is met with varied answers both at the inn where he stays a night and at the church where he meets Father Glaise: 'They were eaten by the wolves', 'They drowned', or 'They were murdered.'

Giorgino is a sombre experience as a film but a compelling one. Images haunt you and take residence in your mind long after you have seen the film: the bleak and wintry wilderness where a single horse and carriage trek through the snow symbolically predicting the madness and loneliness that await Valli. Contrasting with this imagery is the sight of Catherine, a vulnerable, beautiful child in a woman's body. If you fall asleep during the 170 minute running time, you may wake up and think you are having a nightmare.

Jeff Dahlgren is rarely off the screen as Giorgino and is as wonderfully enigmatic as the story, while Mylene Farmer is simply mesmerising whenever she appears. This is only Dahlgren's second acting appearance, his first having been ten years earlier in an American TV series; he is a guitarist and has been part of Farmer's backing group on her many tours. Farmer is France's singing sensation and has made many musical videos. The director is Louis Boutonnat, Mylene's husband and creator of her popular shows.

RARITY RATING: 3/5
After the film's premiere in France and limited screening, it was panned by the critics and removed from public exhibition by Boutonnat. It has since been released in France on DVD.

Laurent Boutonnat: Music video director and composer of Mylene Farmer's short films, Boutonnat's ventures into feature films have been few, his first being *Ballade de la feconductrice* in 1980 and his next *Giorgino* 14 years later. Now he has made his third feature, *Jacquou le Croquant*, an epic tale, beautifully photographed with a rousing soundtrack. Examining his brief oeuvre gives one a greater insight into Farmer's musical videos which are totally unlike any other pop videos you might have seen, with as much detail put into dramatising the story as into the singing of the song. In the video *Mylene Farmer* there are 12 songs and the one that expounds Boutonnat's themes most is 'Libertine', which musically tells the story of a pistol duel between a man and a woman (Farmer), and the woman killing him and being pursued by the dead man's lover. The scene moves to a lavish setting where men in powdered wigs parade themselves with their women. We see Farmer being given a note by a suitor and leaving with him to make passionate love. When she returns, the woman who has chased her earlier erupts into a jealous rage and they furiously fight until her lover rescues Farmer. The film, like all of Boutonnat's work, is erotic and furiously filled with powerful imagery. *Jacquou le Croquant* comes with the same intensity but minus Mylene Farmer.

THE 1920s

Buster Keaton and Charlie Chaplin immediately come to mind when you mention the 1920s, but it was also the decade that spawned Abel Gance's *Napoleon*, Eisenstein's *Battleship Potemkin*, Murnau's *Sunrise* and brought sound to the screen with Al Jolson in *The Jazz Singer*. Films were made on nitrate, which was highly flammable, and consequently many were reduced to ashes. Time is no discriminator of art, and among the films that have been lost are a Lang, a Hitchcock and a Lubitsch.

Four Around a Woman (Vier um die Frau)   1921

Directed by: Fritz Lang
Written by: Fritz Lang. Thea von Harbou.
Cast: Hermann Bottcher, Anton Edthofer, Robert Forster-Larrinaga, Harry Frank, Ludwig Hartau.

Story: A merchant named Yquem buys his wife some exquisite jewellery in part of the city that trades in fake and stolen goods. He sees a man with whom his wife had an affair. Following the man to a hotel, he writes a letter to him copying his wife's handwriting and inviting him to a public area where Yquem will spy on them and try and discover whether they still love each other.

Lang had already scored a remarkable triumph with *Metropolis* when he took this excursion into melodrama. There are great scenes contrasting the aristocratic opulence of the manor houses with the wretchedness of the grimy gutters of the slums. Good performances all round, but particularly from Rudolf Klein-Rogge who was later to star in another Lang classic *Dr Mabuse*.

RARITY RATING: 4/5
Surprisingly a print turned up at the Cinematica De Sao Paulo in Brazil a few years ago, so there is a chance that the British Film Institute or the American Film Institute might screen it some day.

Fritz Lang: Austrian-born film director Lang achieved Hall of Fame notoriety with the silent film classic *Metropolis* and the dark thriller *M*, which told of a notorious child killer played by Peter Lorre. The latter film, once seen, haunts the memory due to Lorre's remarkable performance. Based on the real-life case of a Dusseldorf murderer, a sexual psychopath who murders little girls, Lorre captured all the complexities of such a killer and at the same time allowed the viewer to see his own suffering. 'I can't help myself,' he screams at the police. It was Lang's first sound film and firmly established him as a name synonymous with class. He brought the same atmospheric film noir style with him America where he made films like *The Woman in the Window*, *The Big Heat* and *While the City Sleeps*. Lang trained to be a painter but then took up writing, which eventually led to filmmaking. Once offered a job by Nazi propaganda minister Josef Goebbels to head the German Cinema Institute, he refused, and it was offered and accepted by Leni Riefenstahl.

The Mountain Eagle 1926

Directed by: Alfred Hitchcock
Written by: Max Ferner. Charles Lapworth (story).
Cast: Nita Naldi (Beatrice), Malcolm Keen (John Fulton), John F Hamilton (Edward Pettigrew), Bernhard Goetzke (Mr Pettigrew).

Story: Set in Kentucky, *The Mountain Eagle* tells of a storekeeper named Pettigrew (Goetzke) who falls in love with Beatrice (Naldi), a schoolteacher, but unfortunately for him his love is not returned. She runs away and marries a hermit, Fulton (Keen). Out of anger, Pettigrew accuses Beatrice of molesting Edward (Hamilton), his mentally retarded son. When this doesn't work, Pettigrew decides to hide his son and then accuses Fulton of his murder. The innocent hermit is imprisoned for a non-existent crime, but he manages to escape and join his wife and their son in the mountains of Kentucky.

Though it is somewhat dated and carries the burden of Hitchcock having hated it, *The Mountain Eagle* is still entertaining and would be worth seeking out. It has all the hallmarks of Hitchcock's later films: unrequited love, a beautiful woman, and an innocent man wrongly accused of murder.

RARITY RATING: 5/5
A full set of stills exists but sadly no copies of the film.

Alfred Hitchcock: Alfred Hitchcock was one of the few film directors whose name was as well known as the stars who starred in his films, and they were some of the most famous names in Hollywood: Gregory Peck, Ingrid Bergman, James Stewart, Montgomery Clift, Grace Kelly, Cary Grant, Shirley MacLaine, Doris Day, Henry Fonda, Kim Novak, James Mason, Janet Leigh and Paul Newman. A 'Hitchcock film' was guaranteed to deliver suspense in a style that he made his own. Plots were designed to lead the audience astray, a device that Hitch called the MacGuffin. Another distinguishing feature of his films was that he made a brief cameo appearance in all of them from *The Lodger* onwards. It was fun for the cinemagoer to try to spot him as his appearances were wide and varied. He was seen in a newspaper office in *The Lodger*, carrying a stick in *Easy Virtue*, on a subway in *Blackmail*, on a street in *Murder!*, near a music hall in *The 39 Steps*, as a reporter outside a magistrate's court in *Young and Innocent*, at a railway station in *The Lady Vanishes*, outside a phone booth in *Rebecca*, holding a newspaper in *Foreign Correspondent*, passing Mr Smith in *Mr & Mrs Smith*, posting a letter in *Suspicion*, on a train playing cards in *Shadow of a Doubt*, leaving an elevator in *Spellbound*, drinking champagne at a party in *Notorious*, carrying a cello case in *The Paradine Case*, walking in the street after the opening credits of *Rope*, at the Governor's reception in *Under Capricorn*, staring at Eve (Jane Wyman) in *Stage Fright*, boarding a train carrying a double bass in *Strangers on a Train*, crossing the top of a staircase in *I Confess*, winding a clock in the songwriter's apartment in *Rear Window*, sitting next to John Robie on a bus in *To Catch a Thief*, walking past Sam's outdoor exhibition in *The Trouble with Harry*, in a Morocco marketplace in *The Man Who Knew Too Much*, as the voice of the narrator at the beginning of the film in *The Wrong Man*, walking past Elster's office in *Vertigo*, missing a bus in *North by Northwest*, wearing a cowboy hat in *Psycho*, leaving a pet shop with dogs in *The Birds*, leaving an office in *Marnie*, in a hotel lobby with a baby in *Torn Curtain*, in a wheelchair at the airport in *Topaz*, as a spectator at the opening rally in *Frenzy*, and as a silhouette at the office in *Family Plot*. Hitchcock's famous silhouette appeared at the beginning and end of his long-running TV series *The Alfred Hitchcock Hour*, aired during the mid-1960s.

Hitch was an EastEnder, born in Leytonstone, London, the son of a greengrocer. His interest in movies began while working as an estimator for the Henley Telegraph and Cable Company, when he frequently visited the local cinema and habitually read the *Hollywood Reporter*. When in 1920 Famous Players Lasky's film studio opened in London, Hitch got a job as a title designer, creating designs for all the films made at the studio over the next two years. In 1922 he directed his first film *Number 13*, which was never completed. His first completed feature was *Always Tell Your Wife*, which Hitch directed when the original director, Hugh Croise, fell ill. In 1929 Hitch directed Britain's first sound film *Blackmail*.

See: *Downhill*.

Downhill   1927

Directed by: Alfred Hitchcock
Written by: Constance Collier (play). Ivor Novello (play).

Cast: Ivor Novello (Roddy Berwick), Robin Irvine (Tim Wakely), Isabel Jeans (Julia), Ian Hunter (Archie), Norman McKinnel (Sir Thomas Berwick), Annette Benson (Mabel), Sybil Rhoda (Sybil Wakely), Lilian Braithwaite (Lady Berwick).

Story: The story of the decline of Roddy Berwick (Novello) from public schoolboy with a bright future to a disgraced alcoholic as a result of taking the blame for his friend Tim (Robin Irvine) getting a shopgirl pregnant. Roddy's downward spiral begins when he is ostracised by his family and severed from his inheritance. He has to find work as an actor and dancer on the stage, a profession looked down upon by higher society. He's kept by an older woman and finally hits total bedrock as he's bundled onto a ship by sailors planning to ransom him back to his parents.

There is a clever and intelligent use of titles by Hitchcock, where only the important dialogue is shown. Novello is ideal for the part and brings his stage experience to the role. There is a cameo by an actress named Daisy Jackson who is simply excellent, but seemingly never appeared again in another Hitchcock film.

RARITY RATING: 4/5
Has cropped up at a few director seasons, but still is unavailable on DVD.

Ivor Novello: In retrospect it might seem a strange choice for a debonair actor and songwriter, playwright and darling of the London stage, to be cast as the lead in a Hitchcock thriller, but Welsh-born (in a village whose name meant Grove of Nightingales) Novello was incredibly versatile. Composing music was his particular forte, and he wrote over 250 songs including the popular *We'll Gather Lilacs* and *Keep the Home Fires Burning*, the patriotic morale-boosting World War One song that was eventually used in the film *The Last Squadron*. As an actor he appeared in his first film *The Call of the Blood* in 1919, but his greatest film success came when he starred in two Hitchcock films: *Downfall* and *The Lodger*. He also became a popular matinee idol of the London stage in *The Rat* and his own successful musicals *Glamorous Night*, *The Dancing Years*, *King's Rhapsody* and *Perchance to Dream*. He remained a prolific writer throughout his career and even wrote the dialogue for the Johnny Weissmuller film *Tarzan the Ape Man* in 1932.

In Robert Altman's film *Gosford Park*, made in 2001, the character of Novello was played by Jeremy Northam. Besides the songs he has left the world, Novello gave his name to the prestigious annual 'Ivor Novello Awards' which are given by the record industry to British publishers, composers and arrangers.

The Patriot   1928

Directed by: Ernst Lubitsch
Written by: Ashley Dukes (play). Julian Johnson (titles).
Cast: Emil Jannings (Czar Paul), Florence Vidor (Countess Osterman), Lewis Stone (Count Paulen), Vera Veronica (Mademoiselle Lapoukaine).

Story: Basically revolves around the madness of Czar Paul, played by one of the cinema's finest actors Emil Jannings who was the first actor to win an Academy Award in its inaugural year for two films: *The Way of All Flesh* and *The Last Command*.

This is one of the most sought after movies by those few who have seen it because it was considered to be Emil Jannings' greatest performance, but also because added talkie sequences were edited into the movie after its first release. The film was nominated for five Oscars: Best Film, Best Actor, Best Director, Best Art Direction and Best Screenplay; it won only the latter.

RARITY RATING: 5/5

No known prints exist. However, Josef von Sternberg took the crowd scenes in *The Scarlet Empress* from *The Patriot*. A trailer for the film was recently rediscovered at The National Film and Sound Archive in Australia. The print was returned to the UCLA Film and Television

Archive where a 16mm print was produced and expatriated back to Screensound in Australia at the request of The Melbourne Cinematheque for Australian screenings.

Ernst Lubitsch: The man whose films became known as having 'the Lubitsch touch', meaning that they displayed a sophistication and humour that reflected aptly the American scene, left his German homeland for Hollywood in 1922. He had by then directed near on 40 films, including two with the great star of the silent screen, Pola Negri: *The Eyes of the Mummy* and *Carmen*. His friend, Mary Pickford, starred in his first American success *Rosita* in 1923, but it took 17 years before Lubitsch really found his lynchpin again when he directed the immortal Greta Garbo in *Ninotchka* with Melvyn Douglas for MGM. The comedy was fast-paced and Garbo shone. In 1942, Lubitsch directed his masterpiece *To Be or Not to Be*, starring Carole Lombard and Jack Benny. It was a vicious black comedy of Nazi tyranny that looked at the problems facing an acting troupe in Poland during wartime occupation, and highlighted Benny's genius delivery of deadpan humour. The last film that Lubitsch made was *Heaven Can Wait*, which featured Don Ameche and Alice Faye. It was to be his last completed work because later that year, 1944, he had a heart attack; what was to have been his next film, *A Royal Scandal*, was finished by Otto Preminger. He will also be remembered for pairing two of the most popular singing stars in screen history: Maurice Chevalier and Jeanette MacDonald.

See: *Monte Carlo, The Smiling Lieutenant.*

THE 1930s

Sound was now the norm as cinema entered the 1930s with Lewis Milestone's epic *All Quiet On the Western Front*, one of the greatest anti-war films of all time, and the decade ended with MGM's long-awaited classic *Gone With the Wind*. Billboards exclaimed that 'Garbo talks!' in *Anna Christie*, while Edward G Robinson was uttering his immortal exit line, 'Is this the end of Rico?' in *Little Caesar*. Charles Laughton was throwing chicken bones over his shoulder in *The Private Lives of Henry VIII* and Bette Davis was waiting to pounce on Leslie Howard in *Of Human Bondage*. Cagney proclaimed, 'What a lovely day for a moider,' in *Angels With Dirty Faces*, and Cary Grant and Irene Dunne blossomed in *The Awful Truth*. But perhaps the greatest legacy that these years gave the cinemagoer was the emergence of the inspiring films of Frank Capra. Nevertheless, there were three John Fords that somehow became ambushed in a stampede for posterity, a couple of Jimmy Stewart films, plus a Barbara Stanwyck that rode off into the sunset.

Monte Carlo   1930

Directed by: Ernst Lubitsch
Written by: Ernest Vajda. Vincent Lawrence (additional dialogue).
Cast: Jack Buchanan (Count Rudolph Falliere), Jeanette MacDonald (Countess Helene Mara), Claude Allister (Prince Von Siebenheim).

Story: Countess Von Conti leaves her bridegroom Prince Von Siebenheim at the altar and takes a train to Monte Carlo. She is admired by a shy womaniser, Count Rudolph Falliere (Buchanan). His attempts to win her approval are marred by his nervousness and bad fortune, but things improve when he poses as a hairdresser and she slowly begins to warm to him.

With a great teaming of MacDonald and Buchanan, the film has all the ingredients of a typical romantic comedy with the 'Lubitsch touch'. Best song is MacDonald's rendering of *Beyond the Blue Horizon*.

RARITY RATING: 5/5
As video sales depend on demand this seems unlikely to make it on to DVD.

Jack Buchanan: British stage star who entered films during the silent era with *Auld Lang Syne*, making a further 34 pictures culminating with the most popular in 1955, *The Band Wagon*, teaming him with Hollywood's Fred Astaire and Cyd Charisse. During the production Buchanan suffered from severe pain due to three dental operations, but he still managed to shine and charm his way through the film. Part of his popularity was due to his creamy-coated voice, which seemed to purr rather than vocalise. In *The Band Wagon*, Buchanan played the part of Jeffrey Cordova, a prolific producer based on the star Jose Ferrer who at the time was producing four Broadway shows and starring in a film. Continual bad health plagued Buchanan, particularly spinal arthritis. It was therefore fitting that, like Astaire, who was nearing the end of a long and successful screen career, Buchanan's filmography should end with a fine and exuberant Vincente Minnelli musical like *The Band Wagon*.

The Smiling Lieutenant 1931

Directed by: Ernst Lubitsch
Written by: Leopold Jacobson (operetta). Felix Dormann (operetta).
Cast: Maurice Chevalier (Lt. Nikolaus von Preyn), Claudette Colbert (Franzi), Miriam Hopkins (Princess Anna), Charles Ruggles (Max).

Story: Based on the operetta by Jacobson and Dormann, Nikolaus von Preyn is an officer of the Austrian royal guard who is utterly smitten with his girlfriend, Franzi, a violinist. Niki has stolen Franzi from her man, Max, but he has to marry Princess Anna.

Delightfully played by Chevalier and Colbert in the leading roles of Niki and Franzi, with fine support from Miriam Hopkins as the Princess and Charles Ruggles as Max. However, the film is almost stolen from all of them by an outstanding performance from George Barbier as King Adolf XV. Overall, another charming picture from Lubitsch, the master of warm comedies.

RARITY RATING: 3/5
Only a renewed interest in Lubitsch will bring this jewel to DVD.

Maurice Chevalier: Youthful activities as a sparring partner for the French heavyweight boxer Georges Carpentier and aspirations to be an acrobat finally led to his chance to enter films. After being captured and imprisoned by the Germans in World War One, he appeared in French films until he was lured to Hollywood in 1928. He made a series of successful musicals with Jeanette MacDonald, including *Love Parade* in 1929 and the even more popular *Love Me Tonight* in 1932. But it was over 20 years later when Chevalier really captured the hearts of American audiences with his role as Honore Lachaille in MGM's *Gigi* opposite Leslie Caron.

Chevalier was the epitome of the Parisian charmer with his perpetual smile and cheeky winking-ness. It is almost impossible to hear the song 'Louise' without instantly wanting to impersonate his French tones. Probably no other performer has reflected happiness as he did.

Air Mail   1932

Directed by: John Ford
Written by: Dale Van Every (story). Frank Wead (story).
Cast: Ralph Bellamy (Mike Miller), Gloria Stuart (Ruth Barnes), Pat O'Brien (Duke Talbot), Slim Summerville (Slim McCune).

Story: An exciting adventure from Ford that preceded his westerns, using airplanes and pilots instead of horses and cowboys. It is a thrill-a-minute ride with the pilots as they risk their lives to get Christmas mail delivered. Mike (Bellamy) flies at the risk of losing his licence because of bad eyesight. Duke (O'Brien) is an exhibitionist and loves showing off with his aerodynamic displays, but alcohol fuels his tank. These daredevils of the air are always on a mission and will get the mail through no matter what. They will die. They will sacrifice their lives for others. They will never give up their mission.

It may seem a little corny as years pass but for its time it is amazingly innovative. Pat O'Brien's performance as Duke is full of bravado and humour. Bellamy wrings every drop of emotion from his character. There is fine support too from Gloria Stuart, Slim Summerville and Russell Hopton.

RARITY RATING: 5/5

Mentioned in a documentary on John Ford which is available on video, but the film has been grounded since its original release and seems unlikely to be seen again.

Ralph Bellamy: Had his own theatre company at the age of 26, nominated for an Oscar for his role in the classic comedy *The Awful Truth*, received an honorary Oscar in 1987 for his contribution to the acting profession, and won Broadway's Tony Award as Best Actor for his portrayal of Franklin Delano Roosevelt in *Sunrise at Campobello*, a role he reprised in the film of the same name in 1960.

Considered by his peers to be one of the most respected and likeable actors in the business, Bellamy often played a character that lost his woman to the male lead in the film. He once told producers that if he couldn't get the girl at the end of the picture, then he should at least be given more money.

It was back in 1933 that Bellamy made his film debut as a gangster in *The Secret Six*, between then and his last role as James Morse in *Pretty Woman*, Bellamy appeared in many memorable roles: opposite Cary Grant and Irene Dunne in *The Awful Truth*, with Gary Cooper in

The Court-Martial of Billy Mitchell, and as Dr Sapirstein in Roman Polanski's *Rosemary's Baby*, but undoubtedly his greatest performance
was as Roosevelt in *Sunrise at Campobello*.

Pilgrimage   1933

Directed by: John Ford
Written by: Barry Conners. Philip Klein.
Cast: Henrietta Crosman (Mrs Hannah Jessop), Heather Angel (Suzanne),
Norman Foster (Jim Jessop), Lucille La Verne (Mrs Kelly Hatfield).

Story: A biblical take in a way that does seem dated but still has moments of interest. It concerns a woman, Hannah Jessop (Crosman),
whose son Jimmy is killed in the war. She always read to him from the
Bible and warned him against evil women. Despite his mother's plead-
ings, Jimmy meets Mary Saunders (Marian Nixon) and before he goes
off to war is told that she is pregnant with his child. Mary's father asks
Hannah to deliver the baby. Days later Hannah receives a telegram
telling her of her son's death. Ten years later, children verbally abuse
Jimmy's son with accusations that he is a bastard. Mary and her son
leave their home for good. Later Hannah finds herself in a similar situation to the one she was in with her son and the culminating scenes
see her visiting his grave and asking for his forgiveness.

A 'weepie', which features good performances from Heather Angel
and Marian Nixon. Further down the cast, playing Mrs Worth, you'll
find the name of Hedda Hopper, remembered today as the Hollywood
gossip columnist of the 1940s and 50s with her regular column, *Under
Hedda's Hat*.

RARITY RATING: 5/5
No known prints of this film have survived.

John Ford: Probably recognised in the industry as having directed more
great films than any other director in living memory. His career spanned

over 60 years in the business from his first silent film to the documentary *Chesty: A Tribute to a Legend*. Identified mainly with westerns, he made one of his most memorable movies in 1939, *Stagecoach*, starring John Wayne and Claire Trevor. He won his first of four Oscars in 1932 for *The Informer*, the others coming for *The Grapes of Wrath*, *How Green Was My Valley* and *The Quiet Man*. Among his other classic westerns were *My Darling Clementine*, *Fort Apache*, *She Wore a Yellow Ribbon*, and what for many is considered to be the greatest western of them all, *The Searchers*, with John Wayne, Jeffrey Hunter and a young Natalie Wood. *The Man Who Shot Liberty Valance* came out in 1962 and starred another of Ford's favourite actors James Stewart teaming him with Wayne and Lee Marvin. Stewart played a lawyer trying to rid his town of bad man Liberty Valance, played by Marvin. A good enough western to be spoken of in the same reverential breath as *Stagecoach*.

Monument Valley in Arizona/Utah became synonymous with Ford as it appeared in nearly all his westerns. His film philosophy was simple: 'Anybody can direct a picture once they know the fundamentals. Directing is not a mystery, it's not an art. The main thing about directing is: photograph the people's eyes.'

In later years he wore an eye-patch; it covered a blind eye, which was caused when he removed a bandage too soon after cataract surgery.

He was the first recipient of the American Film Institute Life Achievement Award in 1973.

See: *Air Mail*, *The Plough and the Stars*.

Annie Oakley 1935

Directed by: George Stevens
Written by: Joseph Fields (story). Ewart Adamson (story).
Cast: Barbara Stanwyck (Annie Oakley), Preston Foster (Toby Walker), Melvyn Douglas (Jeff Hogarth), Moroni Olsen (Buffalo Bill).

Story: Sharpshooter Annie Oakley (Stanwyck) utilised her charms and grit to rise from the backwoods of America to become famous as the gal who could outshoot the world champion, Toby Walker (Foster), and join Buffalo Bill's Wild West Show. She held the title of the World's Greatest Woman Rifle Shot and became a celebrity the world over. There is some Hollywood licence with history in telling the story, but the charisma of this remarkable film is never lost.

This really is an unsung classic, which showcases the vibrancy and versatility of Stanwyck, who later went on to star in major movies such as *Golden Boy*, *The Lady Eve*, *Double Indemnity* and *Sorry, Wrong Number*. She is utterly convincing as Annie Oakley and totally outshines and outdraws Betty Hutton's attempt at the role in the weaker *Annie Get Your Gun*, which even music couldn't save. George Stevens, who is fondly remembered for the westerns *Shane* and *Giant*, firmly grips the directorial reigns. Annie Oakley was no ordinary woman and this is no ordinary film.

RARITY RATING: 4/5
On rare occasions has appeared on television but is still not available on DVD or VHS.

Barbara Stanwyck: There is no tombstone for Barbara Stanwyck as her ashes were scattered in the wind, but she left us her films as her memorial. Stanwyck was often called the 'Best Actress Who Never Won An Oscar', which is quite fitting when one looks at her filmography. One of her greatest influences was Frank Capra who directed her in *The Bitter Tea of General Yen* and told her: 'Eyes are the greatest tool in film.' It was a lesson that she never forgot. Those eyes burnt fire in *Annie Oakley*, welled tears in *Stella Dallas*, melted hearts in *Meet John Doe*, suggested murder in *Double Indemnity*, showed fear in *Sorry, Wrong Number*. During her lifetime many quotes were attributed to her but none more profound than when she said: 'Egotism – usually just a case of mistaken nonentity.'

She received the American Film Institute Life Achievement Award in 1987 and was inducted into the Hall of Great Western Performers of the National Cowboy and Western Heritage Museum in 1973.

See: *The Plough and the Stars*.

The Plough and the Stars 1936

Directed by: John Ford
Written by: Dudley Nichols
Cast: Barbara Stanwyck (Nora Clitheroe), Preston Foster (Jack Clitheroe), Barry Fitzgerald (Fluther Good), Dennis O'Dea (Young Covey).

Story: All about the Irish rebellion and based on the Sean O'Casey play. Centres on the Clitheroe family, Jack and Nora (Preston Foster and Barbara Stanwyck), and how the Easter Rebellion is affecting their lives. Nora is afraid that her husband will fight for the Irish Republican Army and when a friend, Ned Brennan, brings him a letter telling him to report as a commandant, he leaves immediately.

Though eventually the rebellion is smashed, the rebels keep fighting for the freedom of Ireland.

Both the Fitzgerald brothers, Barry and Arthur Shields, feature in the movie and in real life were Ulster Protestants. Stanwyck's Irish brogue is grating and many of the scenes are played as if they were stage acting, but the chemistry between Foster and Stanwyck is still convincing. All in all it stands the test of time, and it *is* a John Ford film and should be saved.

RARITY RATING: 4/5
The film was once available on video but seems to have faded away. Copies found now would be at a premium.

Preston Foster: Actor, composer, songwriter, author and musician, Preston Foster was – in a nutshell – versatile. Among the songs that he composed was one called 'Got to get my Mojo Working', which was used in the comedy *Meet the Parents*. Few of his films were memorable and he eventually drifted into television work in the 1950s.

Often mistakenly confused with the actor Robert Preston because of a strong resemblance to the star of *The Music Man*, though he was not related.

See: *Annie Oakley.*

Seventh Heaven

Directed by: Henry King
Written by: Melville Baker
Cast: Simone Simon (Diane the Hooker), James Stewart (Chico), Jean Hersholt (Father Chevillon), Gregory Ratoff (Boul the Cab Driver), Gale Sondergaard (Nana).

Story: This is the remake of the Oscar-winning film that starred Janet Gaynor and Charles Farrell and, like most remakes, struggles to live up to the original – but it does. The setting is still Paris but it now has a war to contend with. Chico (Stewart) saves a prostitute, Diane (Simon), from suicide and being arrested, and takes on a personal mission to guide her to have faith so that she can have a new life. His ambitions are simple: he wants to leave his job as a sewer worker and become a street cleaner. He also wants to meet and marry a beautiful woman – he achieves it all.

This is a very uplifting movie and, in the capable hands of cinema's eternal optimist Jimmy Stewart, it is totally believable. As always he knows how to squeeze a tear from the eye and a hug from the heart. He teams expertly with Simone Simon and they illuminate the darkest moments. An example of their charismatic chemistry is seen when Chico looks at her for the first time and, as she returns his look, we hear her musical theme played, 'Diane', without which I am sure we would have heard their heartbeats. Simone Simon was an extraordinary beauty who captivated many hearts but not many good scripts. She returned to France and featured in numerous films there. The lucky few who have seen her in this film will never forget it.

RARITY RATING: 4/5
Once flickered on our television screens but that was a long, long time ago.

Simone Simon: French actress whose popularity was greater in her own country where she made 50 per cent of her films. Internationally, she is remembered as the eponymous Cat in *Cat People*, a film that has earned itself cult status among cinephiles. The film was produced by Val Lewton and set a higher standard for the horror genre with its film noir style and setting. *Cat People* greatly influenced other filmmakers, particularly Hitchcock, and this can be seen in the shower sequence from *Psycho*. Simon later reprised her role of Irene Reed in the sequel made two years later, *Curse of the Cat People*.

Working twice with the great director, Max Ophuls, in *Le Voleur* and *La Ronde*, and once under the direction of Jean Renoir in *La Bête humaine*, Simone Simon honed her craft to become a very good actress. Her sensuous charm and ability to captivate an audience can be witnessed in the neglected classic *The Devil and Daniel Webster*, in which she played the role of Belle, a dancer to tempt the devil.

See: *The Sad Sack*, *Le Voleur*.

It's a Wonderful World   1939

Directed by: WS Van Dyke
Written by: Ben Hecht
Cast: Claudette Colbert (Edwina Corday), James Stewart (Guy Johnson), Guy Kibbee (Fred Streeter), Nat Pendleton (Sergeant Fred Koretz).

Story: Seeing this title reminds me of the joke about a man who tried inventing a soft drink and gave up on his sixth attempt, which he had called 6 Up. This isn't the classic Capra movie, and definitely lacks the *life* of that title and the pure joy of one of the greatest films ever made. *It's a Wonderful World* is really a hodgepodge of a story and, despite the best efforts of its stars, fails to deliver the comedy it promises. Stewart plays a detective trying to discover who framed his friend and then spends most of the time with Colbert trying to escape from the police. On their travels they become involved with an acting troupe and some boy scouts. It is all tirelessly pointless, however, a slapstick comedy without the comedy. Very little to recommend it besides its novelty value, which is cold comfort to its screenwriters who on better days penned the delightful *Thin Man* series.

RARITY RATING: 4/5
It has been seen on television and instantly forgotten.

Claudette Colbert: Came to movies after appearing on Broadway in the early 1920s, transferring her allegiance to films during the Depression when most theatres closed down. She debuted in 1927 in *For Love of Mike* and then went on to make over 70 movies. In 1934 she starred in Cecil B DeMille's biblical epic *Cleopatra* and then Capra's romantic comedy *It Happened One Night* opposite Clark Gable, which collected Oscars for Best Film, Best Director, Best Actor and, of course, Best Actress.

At the end of that decade she starred with Henry Fonda in the classic western *Drums Along the Mohawk*. Five years later Colbert appeared in one of her greatest films *Since You Went Away*, as Anne Hilton, a woman who is comforted by her husband's best friend, Tony, when she is left trying to control her two daughters and an irascible boarder, Colonel Smollett, while her husband is away at war. Teamed with a fine cast of Joseph Cotton, Jennifer Jones, Robert Walker, Shirley Temple and Monty Woolley, the film gained Claudette Colbert a Best Actress nomination for an Oscar.

Colbert preferred to be photographed showing her left profile as she was self-conscious about a bump on her nose caused by an earlier injury.

See: *The Smiling Lieutenant.*

THE 1940s

Crosby, Hope and Lamour teamed up for the first time in a long series of *Road* movies. Orson Welles reinvented the way films are made with his masterpiece *Citizen Kane*. Bogart kissed Bergman goodbye in *Casablanca*, Judy Garland sang 'The Trolley Song' in *Meet Me in St Louis*, Gene Kelly danced with an animated mouse in *Anchors Aweigh*, Widmark pushed a cripple down the stairs in *Kiss of Death*, Celia Johnson got a piece of grit in her eye and Trevor Howard in her heart in *Brief Encounter*, Clarence got his wings in *It's A Wonderful Life*, and Harry Lime came out of the shadows in *The Third Man*. Yes, these really were the Golden Years...

Lost Angel   1943

Directed by: Roy Rowland
Written by: Isobel Lennart. Angna Enters (story).
Cast: Margaret O'Brien (Alpha), James Craig (Mike Regan), Marsha Hunt (Katie Mallory).

Story: A six-year-old child is left on the doorstep of a scientific institution and is groomed to be a genius by three professors, played by Philip Merival, Henry O'Neill and Donald Meek. A police reporter, James Craig, meets the child and takes charge of her; he begins to de-programme her so that she can have a normal upbringing. His girlfriend, a nightclub singer, also becomes fond of her. A subplot involves a group of gangsters.

Margaret O'Brien steals the film with her astonishing gift as an actress. She had the ability to cry on cue and challenged her co-stars to be at their very best. A true star draws you to them like a magnet; when they are on screen it's impossible to watch anyone else. O'Brien had that quality and the fact that she was only six years old at the time of this film is even more remarkable. Keen viewers will recognise the hat-check girl to be Ava Gardner.

RARITY RATING: 3/5
Can be seen on satellite television and is part of Turner's Classic Movies. Never released on DVD.

Margaret O'Brien: A naturally talented actress who entered films at the age of four and continued to be a scene-stealer until her early teens. She never gained the same popularity as an adult that she had as a child actress, when she simply became one of the best infant ingénues in the business. In retrospect, her early films like *Journey For Margaret*, made when she was five, stand the test of time and are a great example of her exemplary genius. She changed her name from Angela O'Brien to Margaret after the success of *Journey For Margaret*. In 1944, in her tenth film, *Meet Me in St Louis*, Margaret won an Academy Award for her performance as Tootie. Her last significant screen role was as Mary Lennox in *The Secret Garden*. Though she surfaced briefly at the age of 19 in *Glory*, she spent the rest of her career acting on the small screen in TV dramas.

The Rich Full Life 1947

Directed by: Robert Z Leonard
Written by: Harold Buchman
Cast: Elizabeth Taylor (Cynthia Bishop), George Murphy (Larry Bishop), SZ Sakall (Professor Rosenkrantz), Mary Astor (Louise Bishop).

Story: From the play of the same title – the film was called *Cynthia* on its release in America – *The Rich Full Life* is a great vehicle for the then

15-year-old Elizabeth Taylor who plays a girl who has never had a date. We see her through her first high-school dance and her first romance. We learn that her parents, Larry and Louise, have sacrificed their personal dreams because of Cynthia. She is given music lessons with a Professor Rosenkrantz and attended by the best doctor: Dr Fred I Jannings (Gene Lockhart). Her health is so fragile that she is only allowed to go down to the corner store. All of this on top of the vicissitudes and traumas of the average teenage girl.

Even today I still remember the warm glow that this film projected, akin to watching a favourite movie on Sunday afternoon. Nostalgically treasured but unfortunately carelessly neglected by TV programme directors and DVD distributors today.

RARITY RATING: 4/5
May re-appear some day in a cinema's retrospective of Taylor's oeuvre, but don't hold your breath.

Elizabeth Taylor: One of the best-known names in films, with a career in the industry for over 50 years, beginning at the age of ten in *One Born Every Minute* and culminating at 62 in *The Flintstones*. In 1944, Elizabeth played Velvet Brown in MGM's *National Velvet*, opposite Mickey Rooney. The film catapulted Taylor to fame and she became MGM's most popular child star. One of her closest friends was Montgomery Clift who she starred with in *A Place in the Sun* and *Raintree County*. When Clift had his disfiguring car accident in the early 1950s, Liz was the first on the scene to pull him from the wreckage. As for her married life, it was far less stable than her film persona. Married eight times, twice to Richard Burton, Elizabeth Taylor was tragically parted from the one man who seemed ideally suited to her, Mike Todd, who was killed in a plane crash after only being married to her for 13 months.

She won two Oscars in her career, the first for her role as Gloria Wandrous, a call girl involved with a married man, in the film *Butterfield 8*. Her second Oscar came six years later for the part of gin-swilling Martha in the filmed version of Edward Albee's award-winning play *Who's Afraid of Virginia Woolf?* opposite her husband at the time, Richard Burton.

She became the first film star to be paid a million dollars for her role as *Cleopatra*. Besides the aforementioned films, Elizabeth's acting prowess was also to the fore in two films based on plays by Tennessee Williams, *Cat on a Hot Tin Roof* and *Suddenly Last Summer*, as well as her performance as Lesley Benedict in *Giant* alongside co-star James Dean.

Perhaps she was recognising that the childlike quality she had brought to her films had somehow transferred itself to her personal life, when she said at the age of 53: 'I think I'm finally growing up – and about time too.'

The Upturned Glass   1947

Directed by: Lawrence Huntington
Written by: Pamela Mason. John P Monaghan (story).
Cast: James Mason (Michael Joyce), Rosamund John (Emma Wright), Pamela Mason (Kate Howard), Ann Stephens (Ann Wright).

Story: A tormented surgeon, Michael Joyce (Mason), relates the story of an affair he had with a married woman, Emma Wright (John), and a crime committed. She had fallen out of a window, but was she pushed or did she commit suicide? He seeks to take revenge on his lover's sister, Kate Howard (Kellino). But everything does not go to plan. Joyce ends the movie on the edge of a cliff. 'There is no certitude, nor peace, nor help for pain.'

One of Mason's most personal movies, he produced it and his wife, Pamela Kellino, wrote the script. Almost before its time in the way the film is structured and, particularly for a British movie, not willing to tick all the boxes and tie up loose ends. Here nothing is definite. Was it murder? Was it suicide? You decide.

RARITY RATING: 3/5
Not available on DVD or VHS.

James Mason: Yorkshire born, Mason was one of two British stars of the era – the other was Stewart Granger – to successfully transfer his talents to Hollywood, and they travelled well. Mason was generally cast as the villain due to his quiet, mellifluous voice and sinister countenance. Like most British actors he started his acting career on the stage and it was at the Old Vic that he was offered a small role in a film by Alexander Korda. It was an illustrious career that got him nominated three times for an Oscar. Like Stroheim he practically became 'the man you love to hate' in films like *I Met a Murderer*, *The Man in Grey* and *Fanny by Gaslight*. He cruelly hissed the name Francesca, while thrashing at her fingers with a cane to show his displeasure at her piano playing in *The Seventh Veil*. Two of his finest screen performances were in films by Sir Carol Reed: *Odd Man Out*, playing an IRA fugitive, and as Ivo Kern in *The Man Between*, a man once again on the run and very much in *The Third Man* mould. Living in the shadow of one of the best films of all time, *The Man Between* is fondly remembered as a great thriller due mainly to the dynamic chemistry between Mason and his co-star Claire Bloom.

In real life Mason was a well-liked and generous man. He encouraged many actors, notably giving Sam Neill his chance in films. He also discovered several reels of film featuring Buster Keaton in his Hollywood mansion and immediately set about restoring them.

See: *The Story of Three Loves.*

I Walk Alone   1948

Directed by: Byron Haskin
Written by: Theodore Reeves (play). Robert Smith (adaptation).
Cast: Burt Lancaster (Frankie Madison), Lizabeth Scott (Kay Lawrence), Kirk Douglas (Noll Turner), Wendell Corey (Dave).

Story: A convict, Frankie Madison (Lancaster), is released from jail after serving 14 years for taking the rap for a bootlegging crime, having agreed that after his sentence he will become equal business partners with fellow hood Noll Turner (Kirk Douglas). But when Frankie discovers that Noll has since become a successful nightclub owner and that he has been conned out of his share of the business, he contacts an old member of the gang to beat up Noll. It all goes wrong. Kay (Lizabeth Scott), Noll's girlfriend, is embittered by the way Frankie has been treated and leaves her lover. She softens up Frankie and makes him see there is another way to live aside from killing.

Based on a play, and too dialogue-heavy, it is still an entertaining thriller in true film noir fashion. Lancaster and Douglas bounce off each other well, and Corey as Frankie's younger brother, Dave, is outstanding. Not the best of this genre by any means, but undoubtedly a film that should be seen.

RARITY RATING: 3/5
Watch it on Turner Classic Movies if you can.

Burt Lancaster: Biceps and pearly whites, and a laugh that could transform a frown into a smile, Lancaster came charisma-coated and lit up the darkness whenever he walked into a scene. The characters he played, from Swede Andersen to Doc 'Moonlight' Graham, were mesmerising and memorable. Sure there were a few turkeys in his oeuvre but the ones that sparkle outshine the dross. His earlier athletic prowess as a circus acrobat was used to great advantage in *The Flame and the Arrow* and *The Crimson Pirate*; and eventually employed by Carol Reed against the backdrop of a real circus in *Trapeze*. Some of Lancaster's best work was done in movies that were directed by top-notch filmmakers: Fred Zinnemann – *From Here To Eternity*, Alexander MacKendrick – *Sweet Smell of Success*, Louis Malle – *Atlantic City*, Bill Forsyth – *Local Hero*, Luchino Visconti – *The Leopard*. He even directed two films in which he starred: *The Kentuckian* and the lost and forgotten *The Midnight Man*. Of directing, Lancaster said: 'It's the best job in the picture business because, when you're a director, you're God. And you know that's the best job in town.'

The grouchy character played by Walter Matthau in *The Bad News Bears* was based on Lancaster and written by his son Bill. In 1993, while visiting actor Dana Andrews, who was suffering from Alzheimer's, he had a severe stroke that left him incapacitated and unable to speak until his death.

His screen persona was justly recognised and encapsulated in his character Starbuck in *The Rainmaker* when he tells Earl Holliman's character, 'Whenever you get the feeling, you bang the drum'. Lancaster could have been talking about acting and film because he embodied them with passion. 'We're all forgotten sooner or later, but not films. That's all the memorial we should need or hope for.'

See: *The Midnight Man*.

The Great Gatsby 1949

Directed by: Elliott Nugent
Written by: Owen Davis (play). F Scott Fitzerald (novel).
Cast: Alan Ladd (Jay Gatsby), Betty Field (Daisy Buchanan), Macdonald Carey (Nicholas Carraway), Ruth Hussey (Jordan Baker), Barry Sullivan (Tom Buchanan).

Story: Scott Fitzgerald's novel brought to the screen with Alan Ladd as Jay Gatsby, tracing his rise and fall from the poor boy who never dreamed he deserved much from life, to the young man dazzled by wealth, the tough-guy racketeer, and finally the sartorially elegant man of opulence. Set in the jazz era of the 1920s, *The Great Gatsby* evokes an ambience of mystery and excitement, power and poverty. It needed a strong and convincing Gatsby to pull it off and it found that in Ladd.

Sometimes the film loses itself in its own applause, but overall this is a far better movie than the 1974 remake with Redford. Shelley Winters is outstanding as Myrtle Wilson, the neurotic, hypersensitive wife of Wilson (Howard De Silva), who is menacingly morose. Elisha Cook Junior plays the wide-eyed and vulnerable Klipsringer and electrifies with every entrance he makes. But the candle on the Gatsby cake is Ladd himself, who manages to bring to the role every trick he has learnt and more.

Gatsby is meant to be an enigma and Ladd so convincingly plays the part that it is hard to tell the dividing line between the actor and the character. Excellent.

RARITY RATING: 4/5
Unbelievably lost.

Betty Field: In only her second film, *Of Mice and Men*, in the part of Mae, the girl accidentally killed by Lenny, Betty Field established herself as a formidable find in acting terms. And so she proved, as her career highlights: Cassandra in *Kings Row*, Daisy in *The Great Gatsby*, Flo Owens in *Picnic*, Grace in *Bus Stop*, Nellie Cross in *Peyton Place*, Mrs Fanny Thurber in *Butterfield 8*, Stella in *Birdman of Alcatraz*, Ellen in *Coogan's Bluff*. Interspersed were some mediocre roles and a few television dramas, but these parts were significantly strong to prove her mettle as an actress of standing.

She once said of herself, 'I'm not an outstanding personality and I'm certainly no beauty. Acting ability is all I've got to trade on.' For Betty Field, as her films show, she traded well.

Black Magic   1949

Directed by: Gregory Ratoff
Written by: Charles Bennett
Cast: Orson Welles (Cagliostro), Nancy Guild (Marie Antoinette), Akim Tamiroff (Gitano).

Story: Dumas Jr visits his father, Alexandre, in Paris in 1848. The great writer is disturbed by the hypnotic powers of a nineteenth-century charlatan named Cagliostro and claims that the man is writing Dumas's latest work, not him. 'He is a devil, a mountebank, fool.' He tells his son that Cagliostro is not his real name and that his parents were gypsies. Joseph, the boy's name, had a mother who claimed to be clairvoyant. At a gypsy fair she had looked into the eyes of a farmer's baby and foretold its illness. A few days later the child died and Joseph's parents were brought to trial. The charge was that Joseph's mother was a sorceress and they were condemned to death by hanging. Because of the boy's outcry in court at his parents' sentence, he is sentenced to be whipped and, if he survives, for his eyes to be taken out. He does not die, but is saved from disgorging by a family friend, Gitano, and his gang. Gitano tells the boy that he must forget what he has seen, but Joseph says he will always remember the man who condemned his parents – de Montagne!

The boy grows up into a devil-may-care vagabond. He is next heard of in Vienna in a gypsy caravan presenting a show of black magic and a curio that he claims is the elixir of life. An incident causes a woman to be taken ill and Joseph heals her by hypnotising her pain away. A riot occurs because someone plants some jewellery and then claims that the gypsies are thieves, but while the fracas continues a man in the crowd questions the woman who has been healed. He is a doctor named Franz Mesmer, and he visits Joseph and Gitano who are now in jail. They are granted bail under Mesmer's supervision and he begins studying the hypnotic powers of Joseph Bitano. As a further demonstration of his powers, Mesmer brings in a man who is suffering from palsy and watches as Joseph cures him by hypnosis. However, Joseph declines Mesmer's offer of partnership and, taking the 500 gold pieces left by the palsy sufferer, returns to his gypsy friends. He tells Gitano and Zoraida that they will no longer go on the road selling bottles of elixir and performing magic, but that their lives will change, as will his name. He declares that he will no longer be called Joseph Bitano and looks up to the sky at a distant star that his mother told him about. 'My name will be Cagliostro.'

And so Cagliostro travels, healing, curing the blind and the sick. He becomes a legend. Through the great cities he goes, selling himself as a god. His attitude to the crowds that gather is: 'They cheer you or lash you. It is the same emotion.' Cagliostro decides to return to France and there he meets once more his nemesis, de Montagne, who is seeking a doctor to heal his wife. When Cagliostro sees her he is captivated by her beauty and senses that her illness has been caused by shock. He puts her into a trance and tells her to tell him of the events that led her to the place she is at now...

It was in Strasbourg; King Louis and Marie Antoinette are staying in town. 'I am riding in a carriage with my chaperone when approached by a stranger who then apologises and hastily retreats. I discover that his name is Chambord and he is in the employ of one de Montagne. Then another made the same mistake. That afternoon Chambord took me to the palace and showed me the person they had mistaken me for: Marie Antoinette. Later in the gardens when I was with Chambord, a group of men appeared out of nowhere and my love fought them with his sword but they overpowered him and took me away.' Cagliostro asks her if there was a plot to use her likeness to the Queen. She answers that there was and that it came from a high personage in Paris. Cagliostro tells her to go back to sleep and only to waken at the sound of his voice. He tells de Montagne that he knows of his plan to use the girl to impersonate the Queen and that without his help the girl will die. He insists that he take her with him and demands the fee of 5,000 francs for his services. De Montagne reluctantly agrees but in addition Cagliostro asks for introduction to the court of Louis XVI in return for caring for the girl.

A palace guard is looking for the girl but Cagliostro and Gitano manage to escape with her. In Paris, Cagliostro's fame eclipses anything that he has previously known. But soon Chevalier arrives at the Cagliostro residence, demanding to see the girl who he calls Lorenza. He accuses them of abduction. Zoraida pleads with Cagliostro not to go to the girl but he pushes her away. He uses his power over Lorenza to manipulate her mind so that she loves him. His hypnotic influence over her is powerful enough to obliterate memories of anyone else she may have loved. When she wakes from the trance she thinks she has been dreaming and he asks what she dreamt. That she loved him? She was in his arms? She protests that it was not so. Cagliostro tells her that she is free to go, there is nothing stopping her. She answers: 'Only your eyes.' And he realises that she doesn't really love him but carries another in her heart.

De Montagne calls on him with Madame du Barry, who wants to see the woman who looks like 'the Austrian baggage!' When she sees her she is astounded by the likeness to Marie Antoinette. Du Barry tells Cagliostro that his name is included to attend court and he will then see the real Antoinette. She reminds him that he is a partner in their scheme to substitute Lorenza for the real Queen of France. 'Louis would marry me tomorrow if it wasn't for this… woman.' Cagliostro has now achieved what he desired at the illustrious court of France and met Marie Antoinette. On seeing Cagliostro, Marie Antoinette proclaims to Louis, 'You see, now she brings her witch doctor to court.' The court announces the presence of Louis, the king of France, and Countess Antoinette. It has been arranged that a group of 'guinea pigs' be brought in to test Cagliostro's healing powers. Louis asks him to cure them all at once. Cagliostro is willing to oblige. But it is a trick that is being played on him and one of the group stands up and shouts: 'All we need is one look from you and we are all cured!' And then they start dancing and the entire court is in uproar with Louis laughing the most.

But Cagliostro stops the laughter when he tells Louis, 'If I can heal, then I can also afflict!' He walks to the one who seems to be the leader of the group, stares at him, and tells him to go down on his knees and that he won't be able to get up. 'What was your affliction?' he asks. 'It was supposed to be paralysis,' he answers. He then paralyses him and instantly cures him before the throne of France.

Later, Chambord finds Lorenza and takes her away with him, but they have been spied upon by Zoraida. Meanwhile, her jeweller, who has made a necklace for the Princess, visits du Barry. De Montagne tells Cagliostro that he must make sure that Lorenza will impersonate Antoinette and buy the necklace from the jeweller. And du Barry enthuses that all of France will know that Antoinette has spent one million francs of their money on a necklace! They will find the necklace in her room and Louis will be forced to banish her forever to stop the bloodshed. Cagliostro says that he foresees bloodshed and a new queen of France. He also sees a new minister of finance, the most powerful position of all. He says that the man he sees has a scar on his left hand – de Montaigne. But when Cagliostro returns to Lorenza he finds that she has gone. He forces Zoraida to tell him where. Cagliostro once again has her under his spell and this time he has no intention of letting her go – he marries her. Chambord reaches the church and cannot believe that she has married Cagliostro. In a trance-like state, Lorenza tells him that she loved him once but not anymore.

Du Barry brings news to Cagliostro that King Louis has been stricken with apoplexy. She tells him that the king is dying but that he can save him. But when he asks Louis to open his eyes, he cannot and he dies. An aide sarcastically asks of him, 'Well, sorcerer, can you raise the dead?' Antoinette banishes du Barry from the country and tells Cagliostro that he has one week to leave France. De Montagne forces his way into his home to find Lorenza but is told by Cagliostro that she is dead, an obvious suicide. He insists that her death must be kept secret and that she be buried in Cagliostro's garden. But once de Montagne has left Cagliostro revives Lorenza only to hear her say that she had a dream about Chambord. 'You cannot force her to love you,' says Gitano. Cagliostro sets in motion the most diabolical plot that France has ever seen...

De Montagne receives a letter from Queen Antoinette inviting him to meet her in the Bois de Boulogne. The coach is waiting for him but it carries Cagliostro and Lorenza posing as Antoinette. As de Montagne saw Lorenza buried in the grave he must believe that she is the Queen of France. Under Cagliostro's spell, Lorenza tells de Montagne that she loves him and gives him her ring. She tells him to come to her apartment the next night at midnight and that the guards will be withdrawn. She also asks a second favour: to bring the diamond necklace that the jeweller had made for her. He protests that he would be killed if he agreed to her request. 'You will not die while I am on the throne,' she tells him. The public riot when they hear the news that de Montagne has bought the necklace with money from the public treasury. Chambord is told that Lorenza awaits him; that is part of Cagliostro's plan. Lorenza tells Chambord the plan and that he must intervene to save her life among others. De Montagne, unaware of the plot against him, goes to meet the person he thinks is Antoinette at the palace.

De Montagne and Chambord meet and fight each other until the King, who tells them that they were warned they would be coming to steal the necklace, stops them. Cagliostro also meets Antoinette and she tells all three that they are under arrest. 'On what charges?' he asks. 'Treason against the throne of France,' she replies. Cagliostro hypnotises the guard and escapes from his cell. He then confronts de Montagne in the next cell and casts a spell on him, telling him who he really is, to remember that he hanged his mother, and to imagine the rope – the choking rope. 'See your bed sheets torn into threads, they will do instead of a rope for you.' De Montagne hangs himself and Chambord escapes.

With de Montagne dead there is no one it seems to pardon Antoinette. Until one of the ministers brings in two women: Zoraida and Lorenza, who reveal everything about the conspiracy brought about by Cagliostro. The Queen asks Lorenza if she would be willing save her and France by testifying against him in court. She says that she would. When she is called to testify against Cagliostro, he once again casts his spell over her and she cannot do it. Cagliostro plays to the crowd who are on his side and implores the Queen, asking her if this is a trial or an inquisition? When Lorenza faints, he asks for a recess. During the recess, Cagliostro clearly demonstrates to Gitano that he is going mad and he declares himself to be God! But the prosecution has a surprise witness; they call in Dr Franz Mesmer, who is allowed to interrogate Cagliostro and in so doing hypnotises him with the diamond necklace. Mesmer gets him to confess to every crime that he has committed. But with Gitano's aide he escapes to the roof taking Antoinette with him as hostage. Chambord follows and they fight to the death, with Chambord killing Cagliostro with his sword. Finally, at long last, the lovers are reunited as Lorenza waits for him in the grounds.

For most of the film, Welles as Cagliostro has the audience under his spell in a role that was made for him. A known magician himself, he always used the cinema to perform his magic, describing film as 'a ribbon of dreams' and 'the best train set that a boy had ever had'. We cinemagoers have been intrigued and thrilled as we travelled on the train of his thoughts, through his celluloid tunnels: *Touch of Evil, Citizen Kane, The Magnificent Ambersons, The Lady from Shanghai, Macbeth, Othello, The Trial, Chimes At Midnight, The Immortal Story* and *F for Fake*. Was he a genius? As one person said of him, 'There but for the grace of God, goes God!' *Black Magic* is about trickery and has now disappeared without the obligatory puff of smoke, and only time will tell if its magic will be strong enough for it to reappear.

RARITY RATING: 4/5

The box is empty though fakirs have manifested pirated copies.

Orson Welles: He was responsible for making the most innovative, and what many critics claim to be the greatest, film of all time, *Citizen Kane*. He portrayed one of the most charismatic rogues ever to appear on film yet was on screen for only ten minutes, but then the film was *The Third Man*, the character was Harry Lime, and the man was Orson Welles.

Welles was an actor, writer, film director, producer, editor, costume designer, cinematographer, magician. He needed a large body to hold all that talent but, as he was also a gourmet with an insatiable appetite, the self-indulgence provided ample capacity. As he was once quoted as saying, 'My doctor told me to stop having intimate dinners for four, unless there are three other people.'

When Welles made *Citizen Kane* he threw the rulebook for film-making away. He came from theatre and radio where he controlled practically everything, and expected to do the same with film. On *Citizen Kane* he began placing lighting where he wanted it, to achieve the best effects. There were moments when he wanted to show Kane in his youth as a vibrant, dynamically ambitious young man, which he achieved by using high-key lighting. Later, when Kane is older and cynical, he shot harshly so that contrasting shadows loomed everywhere. Lighting was used symbolically to show impending doom, for example when Kane signs the document of declaration and his face plunges into shadow.

Deep focus was employed so that the audience could choose what to watch within a scene, selecting from multiple images or characters within the frame. And of course Welles had the veteran cinematographer Gregg Toland to adjust and perfect the brash new kid's ideas. They also introduced crane shots to make an after-statement: the camera rises up and away from the figure of Susan on stage singing, and up and up to the catwalk above her where two stagehands are looking down on her performance. They look at each other and one of them holds his nose as if to say, 'She stinks'.

Welles also introduced a new cinematic revelation, using sound as a transition from one scene to another, having a character start a sentence in one shot and finish it in the next. All of this was a unique way of telling a story and it was to be Welles' trademark and calling card. After all, he had discovered the biggest electric train set a boy ever had.

Many of the cast of *Citizen Kane* – Cotten, Moorehead, Collins, Colouris and Stewart – were from the Mercury Theatre, Welles' repertory company in Dublin, and he used most of them again in his second film *The Magnificent Ambersons*, a story about a young man's descent from aristocrat to proletarian. Welles lost a lot of control over the film to RKO and their intervention is apparent in the final version that was released to the public. Unfortunately, he was never given carte blanche in any projects again and his films suffered as a result of that decision. However, even a mere glimpse of his genius is better than none at all, and it was still evident in films such as *The Lady from Shanghai* with the multiple mirrors sequence, the long tracking shot that opens *Touch of Evil*, the skilful editing of *F for Fake*.

He has been portrayed on the screen by actor Vincent D'Onofrio in *Ed Wood* and *Five Minutes, Mr Welles*, Liev Schreiber in *RKO 281*, Edward Edwards in *Rita Hayworth: The Love Goddess*, Eric Purcell in *Malice in Wonderland*, Angus Macfadyen in *Cradle Will Rock*, Danny Huston in *Fade to Black* and on television by Paul Shenar in *The Night That Panicked America*, which was a dramatised version of Welles' radio drama *War of the Worlds*. Broadcast in 1938, it caused nationwide panic, convincing many listeners to vacate their homes, believing that Earth had been invaded by Martians.

Another project was his film *The Other Side of the Wind*, starring John Huston, which ran into legal difficulties after it was made. The film is now going to be made by Welles' lifelong friend Peter Bogdanovich and should be released in 2008.

Welles always wanted the last word on his films, and as he rightly said, 'A film is never really good unless the camera is an eye in the head of a poet.'

THE 1950s

Gloria Swanson was ready for her close up in *Sunset Boulevard*, Robert Walker was conspiring murder in *Strangers on a Train*, Warners promised a lion in your lap with 3-D in *Bwana Devil*, Gene Kelly kicked at puddles in *Singin' in the Rain*, Lee Marvin threw hot coffee in Gloria Grahame's face in *The Big Heat*, while Marilyn Monroe reminded men that diamonds were a girl's best friend in *Gentlemen Prefer Blondes*. Bogart clicked ball-bearings while contemplating strawberries in *The Caine Mutiny*, Sinatra crooned with Crosby in *High Society*, Deborah Kerr didn't keep her appointment at the Empire State in *An Affair to Remember*, Tony Curtis matched Burt Lancaster in *Sweet Smell of Success*, Audrey Hepburn took an oath in *The Nun's Story* and Cary Grant was chased by a crop-sprayer in *North by Northwest*. It was a platinum period for movies, yet there were escapees that included three films by Rudoph Maté, a Kazan, a Zinnemann, a Cukor, a Ray, a brilliant screenplay by Chayefsky, and two Kirk Douglas movies. They are out there somewhere...

I'll Get By   1950

Directed by: Richard Sale
Written by: Robert Ellis. Pamela Harris (story).
Cast: June Haver (Liza Martin), William Lundigan (William Spencer), Gloria DeHaven (Terry Martin), Dennis Day (Freddy Lee).

Story: Remake of *Tin Pan Alley*, the film has a winning combination of good music and a lovely actress in the lead. Two song peddlers, Spencer and Lee, are struggling to be recognised in the music business and along the way happen to meet two beautiful sisters and fall in love. William Lundigan and Dennis Day played the songsmiths, and June Haver and Gloria DeHaven the singing sisters.

This film really flirted with my heart when I first saw it and fell in love with June Haver. It had some great music, particularly the title song sung by June and trumpeted by Harry James. The latter inspired me to use it as my imaginary band's signature tune. Other songs were *Takin' a Chance on Love*, sung by Gloria DeHaven, *You Make Me Feel So Young*, *The More I See You*, *I've Got a Gal in Kalamazoo*, *There Will Never Be Another You*, *Deep in the Heart of Texas* and *I've Got the World on a String*.

There were a couple of interesting cameo parts that were filled by Jeanne Crain and Victor Mature. And the soldier that danced with June and Gloria was Dan Dailey. Sweet memories. Sad loss.

RARITY RATING: 4/5
Has become almost as rare as the musical genre itself.

June Haver: Haver started in showbiz at the age of six in a local stage production of *Midnight in a Toyshop*, had her first screen test at the age of nine, and at the age of sixteen signed with Fox. In the following year of 1943 she appeared in her first film, *The Gang's All Here*. She rose to fame at the same time as Betty Grable, billed as the girl with the million dollar legs. Haver didn't have million dollar legs, but a million dollar smile. Groomed by Fox to take over from Grable, Haver had other plans and, after making *The Girl Next Door*, left films completely. She entered a convent for a short while and then met actor Fred Mac-Murray whom she married. Besides the lost musical *I'll Get By*, she appeared in her most popular film in 1949, *Look For The Silver Lining*, opposite Gordon MacRae.

Union Station   1950

Directed by: Rudolph Maté
Written by: Sydney Boehm

Cast: William Holden (Det Lt William Calhoun), Nancy Olson (Joyce Willecombe), Barry Fitzgerald (Inspector Donnelly), Lyle Bettger (Joe Beacom).

Story: Joyce Willecombe (Nancy Olson) notices a man on a train carrying a gun. She reports the sighting to a train conductor who seems disinterested but reluctantly reports it to the police. Joyce is met at Chicago's Union Station by the chief of the railroad police Willy Calhoun (William Holden) who discovers that there is a plan to kidnap a blind heiress. One of the kidnappers girlfriends tells Calhoun that the plan is to murder the girl after the ransom is paid. There is a culminating chase in a maze of tunnels that criss-crosses downtown Chicago.

Any crime noir film directed by Maté, who directed the outstanding *D.O.A.*, would arouse interest and a full-scale investigation of its own. There is a thin line between police brutality and the methods used by the criminals as shown in the scene when they threaten to throw a kidnapper in front of a train. Holden wins out in the acting honours here against his nearest rival – Union Station itself.

RARITY RATING: 4/5
Once available on video, but sometimes copies appear on eBay.

William Holden: Nicknamed Golden Boy, a sobriquet that he inherited after he appeared in the film of the same name as Joe Bonaparte, a pugilistic violin player. The film shot Holden to fame but it wasn't until Billy Wilder cast him as the writer in *Sunset Boulevard* that the public began to really take notice. He had a glib way of delivering his lines which made him ripe for comedy and he was cast opposite Judy Holliday in *Born Yesterday*, which was a box-office hit. The 'golden boy' really hit gold as Sefton in *Stalag 17*, winning a Best Actor Oscar for his role as the cowardly prison camp informer. He continued his successful roll in his next picture, which was the (then) sexually controversial *The Moon is Blue*. Suddenly his good looks were in demand and he was starring in films that displayed his assets as a romantic lead, pairing him with Audrey Hepburn in *Sabrina Fair*, Grace Kelly in *The Country Girl* and *The Bridges of Toki Ri*, Jennifer Jones in *Love* is a *Many Splendoured Thing*, and Kim Novak in *Picnic*. David Lean cast him in the war drama *The Bridge on the River Kwai* with Alec Guinness and then he began to take a few knocks and looked like being counted out from the Hollywood ring. But then Sam Peckinpah directed him in the classic western *The Wild Bunch* and he was assured screen immortality.

Holden's real passion in life was animal preservation in Africa, and in the 1970s he purchased a large piece of land there and began an animal sanctuary.

One Way Street   1950

Directed by: Hugo Fregonese
Written by: Lawrence Kimble (story).
Cast: James Mason (Dr Frank Matson), Marta Toren (Laura Thorsen), Dan Duryea (John Wheeler).

Story: A crook named Wheeler has just masterminded a big heist and is holed up in an apartment with his girlfriend Laura, and Ollie, who was shot in the preceding robbery. A doctor named Matson is called to tend to Ollie. He does so, but then manages to escape with the booty and Wheeler's moll to Mexico. There is a lull in the story while it concentrates on Matson's sojourn in Mexico, but everything picks up to knife-edge intensity when he returns to confront his pursuers.

Two actors whose acting skills were weaned on villainy, Mason and Duryea wrestle with stealing scenes from each other in this great thriller. Fregonese was not a familiar name on films noirs – he was too often saddled with westerns – but he did direct Palance in *The Man in the Attic*, so not all was lost; only this film.

RARITY RATING: 4/5
Come on out, wherever you are... Sadly, not available on DVD.

Marta Toren: Never lived long enough to fulfil the promise of being the next Ingrid Bergman as her career ended abruptly at the age of

31 when she suffered a brain haemorrhage. During her short life, Toren desperately wanted to gain stature as an actress but somehow never got the roles that allowed her to show her abilities. Probably her best-known film is *The Man Who Watched The Trains Go By*; like the actress, it seemed very promising but died an early death.

The Silent Voice   1952

Directed by: Rudolph Maté
Written by: Larry Marcus (story). James Poe.
Cast: Loretta Young (Paula Rogers), Kent Smith (John Rogers), Alexander Knox (Dr Clifford), Tommy Rettig (David Larsen).

Story: The logline on the poster* of this movie read, 'If you were Paula, what would you do?' This is Paula's (Loretta Young) dilemma when she accidentally knocks down and injures a child in her car. She decides to try and heal him and teach him to speak again, and eventually passes herself off as his legal guardian. Young delivers an utterly convincing and heartfelt performance.

The film poses questions to the audience: will Paula be caught and punished for her crime? When the boy regains his speech will he implicate her?

RARITY RATING: 5/5
* The American one-sheet is probably the only thing that you can still buy of this movie, which shows the American title of the film as *Paula*.

Rudolph Maté: Maté was a respected cinematographer with films such as *Dodsworth*, *Foreign Correspondent*, *The Pride of the Yankees* and *Gilda* among his honours. He moved into directing in 1931 with *It Had to Be You*, the first of 31 films he helmed. The film that really placed him above the credits was the (now) classic film noir *D.O.A.*, which opens on a character entering a police precinct to report his own murder. There was also *Second Chance*, an underrated thriller, which starred Jack Palance and was released in 3-D. Unfortunately many of his films have been lost.

See: *Union Station, The Mississippi Gambler*.

Act of Love   1953

Directed by: Anatole Litvak
Written by: Alfred Hayes (novel). Joseph Kessel (French dialogue).
Cast: Kirk Douglas (Robert Teller), Dany Robin (Lise Gudayec/Madame Teller), Barbara Laage (Nina).

Story: An American GI falls in love with a destitute French woman in Paris during World War Two. The soldier, Robert Teller, seeks permission to marry the young Parisian, Lise, but his commanding officer refuses and has Teller transferred. Years later, Teller shows up at a resort and sees a sergeant there and asks about Lise. He is told that she had committed suicide. He then visits a room that Lise had told him about that she had loved. In voiceover, she talks to him; it's a poignant, tearjerking moment.

One thing that Kirk Douglas had was good judgement and he could always be relied upon to bring a character to life; in Teller you can feel his sadness and heartache in every breath he takes as he recalls his lover. Dany Robin was an amazing discovery, and grabbed the attention of Hitchcock, a dab hand at choosing beautiful leading ladies, who used her in *Topaz*. She finished her career back in her home country of France before dying with her husband in a fire in 1998. *Act of Love* also introduced Brigitte Bardot in her first English-speaking role as Lise's friend Mimi.

RARITY RATING: 4/5
Has been shown on TCM but it still has not been released on video.

Kirk Douglas: A superstar in every sense of the word, Douglas has dominated the screen for over 50 years. He debuted in 1946 as Walter

O'Neil in *The Strange Love of Martha Ivers* and ended it at the age of 88 in *Illusion*, playing the part of a filmmaker trying to find and reunite with his estranged son. He has often been compared with his actor friend Burt Lancaster, who had the same dynamic personality, strong jaw-line, gnashing teeth, and a manner of delivering lines that could make them sound much more important than they really were. A gifted actor, Douglas appeared in some outstanding films: *Champion*, *Ace in the Hole*, *Detective Story*, and most memorably as a mouthy megalomaniac in the satire on Hollywood, *The Bad and the Beautiful*.

In *Lust for Life*, he played Vincent Van Gogh, the troubled artist, Doc Holliday in *Gunfight at the O.K. Corral*, and Einar, a vicious Viking, in *The Vikings*. But his greatest bequests to immortality were his roles in two films by Stanley Kubrick: *Paths of Glory* and *Spartacus*. The former saw Douglas as Colonel Dax, defending three soldiers for desertion, while in the latter he played the slave gladiator taking on the might of Rome, both in the arena and out of it.

Father of actor Michael, Douglas has supported his career and even purchased the play *One Flew Over The Cuckoo's Nest* for him, which Michael went on to produce with Jack Nicholson in the leading role. In 1995 Kirk suffered a stroke that impaired his speech but despite his disability went on to play the lead in Michael Goorijan's *Illusion*.

Inexplicably, a number of key Douglas films have been lost or discarded and their titles appear in this book.

See: *I Walk Alone*, *The Story of Three Loves*, *The Juggler*.

The Juggler   1953

Directed by: Edward Dmytrk
Written by: Michael Blankfort (novel).
Cast: Kirk Douglas (Hans Muller), Milly Vitale (Ya'El), Paul Stewart (Detective Kami), Joseph Walsh (Yehoshua Bresler).

Story: Hans Muller (Douglas) is a man tormented by his past as a holocaust victim in a concentration camp under the Nazi regime. It is 1949 and Muller is in Israel, his new home, but he cannot forget the horrors he endured. Now claustrophobic, he sees walls imprisoning him. Uniformed men appear to him as torturers, he has nightmares of crossing a minefield and is constantly reminded of being a prisoner by the tattooed number on his arm. Can he ever leave it all behind him? Molly Vitale is the girl who is trying to put the new state of Israel on the map.

Douglas again dominates the film and it is hard to take your eyes off him and not to feel his suffering. First-rate film. Poor restoration.

RARITY RATING: 4/5
Last seen on The History Channel.

Edward Dmytryk: In his long film career, Dmytryk directed some of the biggest names in Hollywood: Kirk Douglas, Humphrey Bogart, Spencer Tracy, Montgomery Clift, Elizabeth Taylor, Marlon Brando, Henry Fonda, Richard Widmark, Alan Ladd and Jane Fonda, and was highly revered in his profession. He was one of the original Hollywood Ten who refused to cooperate with the House Un-American Activities Committee, which resulted in his imprisonment. He finally relented and agreed to list names of people in the industry who he maintained were members of the Communist Party. Of all the films he directed, probably directing Bogart in *The Caine Mutiny* would be recognised as his greatest achievement.

Mississippi Gambler   1953

Directed by: Rudolph Maté
Written by: Seton I Miller
Cast: Tyrone Power (Mark Fallon), Piper Laurie (Angelique Dureau), Julie Adams (Ann Conant), John McIntire (Kansas John Polly).

Story: An honest riverboat gambler, Mark Fallon (Power), is very lucky with women and at the poker table, and also a skilful swordsman. His aim is to bring his high principles to gambling, which is generally considered a scoundrel's game. He sets out with his partner to own a gambling palace where honest games are the rule. His motto is that there is no need to cheat when you are the best in the world. On the trip Fallon becomes involved with two beautiful women, the daughter of an aristocrat and a demanding lady who is determined to win his love.

This is a dashing adventure with Power gambling on his looks and talent, and winning hands down with a royal flush. Piper Laurie is also very competent.

RARITY RATING: 4/5
A winner all the way that surprisingly lost out when it came to DVD distribution.

Tyrone Power: The handsomest actor in Hollywood who often regretted those dark dashing looks and boyish charm; he once proclaimed them a curse, saying that he wished he had had a car accident so that his face would get smashed up and he'd look more like Eddie Constantine. He never did break the mould but instead continued to flutter hearts the world over playing heroes such as the eponymous *Jesse James*, and the swashbuckler Don Diego Vega in *The Mark of Zorro*. He could also have audiences weeping as he did in the biographical *The Eddy Duchin Story*. But it was nine years earlier that Power made his greatest film, *Nightmare Alley*, as Stanton Carlisle, a double-crossing charlatan who cons people who believe he has a telepathic gift out of money.

Strangely the only part that he ever played that really stretched him after *Nightmare Alley* was Leonard Steven Vole in Billy Wilder's *Witness for the Prosecution*, his penultimate film. Little can be seen of Power in his last film *Solomon and Sheba*, as he was replaced by Yul Brynner when he collapsed from a heart attack during a duelling sequence with George Sanders and died on his way to hospital.

Man on a Tightrope 1953

Directed by: Elia Kazan
Written by: Neil Paterson (story). Robert E Sherwood.

Cast: Fredric March (Karel Cernik), Terry Moore (Teresa Cernik), Gloria Grahame (Zama Cernik), Cameron Mitchell (Joe Vosdek).

Story: A circus troupe in Czechoslovakia try to escape from the Communistic regime to freedom in Austria, led by Karel Cernik (March) who questions a roustabout regarding his betrayal of the circus and the people he worked with. Cernik's problems are not only restricted to the bullying ways of communism. He also has to confront immediate family tensions involving his wayward wife, Zama, and a strong-willed daughter, Teresa. They escape across the Iron Curtain border in broad daylight and with one fatality.

Full of visual vignettes and fine acting, this is an exciting and gripping drama that is beautifully directed by one of America's greatest directors Elia Kazan. It has a climax that just about rips your heart out and proves what a true actor Fredric March was. Memorable.

RARITY RATING: 5/5
Why a work of such great power and truth has been under lock and key, and refused release on DVD, baffles me.

Elia Kazan: Turkish-born and a proponent of the method style of acting as developed by Stanislavski, Kazan became one of America's finest film directors. He acted himself in six films and was Francis Ford Coppola's first choice to play Hyman Roth in *The Godfather, Part II*. Ultimately the part went to Lee Strasberg, head of the New York School of Method Acting. Kazan's long association with playwright Tennessee Williams resulted in him directing the screen version of *A Streetcar Named Desire*, which catapulted its star Marlon Brando to fame, and steering Carroll Baker into the spotlight as the nymphet *Baby Doll*, based on Williams' play *27 Wagonloads of Cotton*.

Though directing only 21 films, the list of classics is astounding, from *Boomerang* starring Dana Andrews in 1947 to *The Last Tycoon* in 1975. Two of his films won him Academy Awards for best direction: *Gentlemen's Agreement*, 1947, and the film that is remembered more than any other, *On the Waterfront*. Gadge, as he was called by his friends, so-called because of his penchant for gadgetry, was an actor's director and he worked with the best: Katherine Hepburn, Gregory Peck, Richard Widmark, Vivien Leigh, Marlon Brando, James Dean, Montgomery Clift, Natalie Wood, Warren Beatty, Kirk Douglas, Robert De Niro, Jack Nicholson and Robert Mitchum. Like them, he was the best.

That said, during the early 1950s, Elia Kazan testified before the House Un-American Activities Committee, describing the political leanings of his friends and professional associates, which resulted in many of them being ostracised from Hollywood.

The Story of Three Loves   1953

Directed by: Vincente Minnelli. Gottfried Reinhardt.
Written by: John Collier. George Froeschel.
Cast: Kirk Douglas (Pierre Narval), Pier Angeli (Nina Burkhardt), Leslie Caron (Mademoiselle), Farley Granger (Thomas Clayton), James Mason (Charles Coutray), Moira Shearer (Paula Woodward).

Story: An omnibus film of three episodes. *The Jealous Lover* opens with Charles Coutray (Mason), a ballet producer who is approached by a fan, causing him to relate a story of the time when he met the greatest ballerina he has ever known, Paula Woodward (Shearer). There is a moment when Coutray is watching Woodward dance and is totally overwhelmed and awestruck by her performance. The second segment, called *Mademoiselle*, is a fantasy about a boy who wishes to grow up so that he can be rid of his French governess played by Leslie Caron. His wish is granted for four hours and, as an adult (played by Farley Granger), he falls in love with his governess. The final story, *Equilibrium*, concerns an ex-trapeze artist, Pierre Narval (Kirk Douglas), who saves a young woman named Nina (Pier Angeli) from suicide and trains her to become a high-wire performer.

The weakest segment is *Mademoiselle* directed by Minnelli, which fails to convince. The best is undoubtedly *The Jealous Lover* with Mason and Shearer simply superb. While the final episode *Equilibrium*, though starting a little slowly, mounts to an exciting and suspenseful climax. The lesser-known Reinhardt, who is mainly remembered for another Kirk Douglas movie *Town Without Pity*, the title song of which was sung by Gene Pitney and became a hit record for him, directed *The Jealous Lover* and *Equilibrium*.

RARITY RATING: 5/5

It is unlikely to be released to DVD because omnibus films are not considered popular with film enthusiasts.

Pier Angeli: There was a delicacy about Pier Angeli that made the audience fall in love with her yet also want to protect her. She was eventually to take her own life before her 40th birthday. Born in Italy and twin sister of Marisa Pavan, Pier got noticed when she appeared with Kirk Douglas in *The Story of Three Loves*, her sixth film. She went on to appear twice with Paul Newman, in the disastrous *The Silver Chalice* and the excellent boxing biopic of Rocky Graziano, *Somebody Up There Likes Me*. In *Merry Andrew*, she was a welcome distraction from zany Danny Kaye, and, before the good parts totally dried up, she played the role of Anna Curtis, the wife of a man who has been ostracised by his fellow factory workers in Bryan Forbes' *The Angry Silence*. So immersed in the role was she, that in one emotive scene with Michael Craig she left the written script completely and started to holler in Italian. The outburst impressed Forbes so much, that he kept it in the final cut.

The Long Wait 1954

Directed by: Victor Saville
Written by: Alan Green. Lesser Samuels.
Cast: Anthony Quinn (Johnny McBride), Charles Coburn (Gardiner), Gene Evans (Servo), Peggie Castle (Venus).

Story: Based on one of Mickey Spillane's pulp novels, *The Long Wait* is unique, the one story where he abandoned his thuggish hero Mike

Hammer. Instead, in the opening shots we meet a guy called Johnny McBride (Quinn) who hitches a lift, which crashes and bursts into flames. Though McBride survives the accident, he has lost his fingerprints and memory. Eventually he discovers his true identity as the murderer of a district attorney who was prosecuting him for embezzling a quarter of a million dollars. He is released because he has no fingerprints, but others want him dead. McBride has another quest too: to find the girl he once loved. He meets with four possible women who claim his love: Venus, Wendy, Carol and Troy. A typical noir setting is evoked when Venus crawls across the floor to McBride under the pretence of kissing him but really to steal his gun.

Memorable for the macho Quinn and a song sung over the title credits called 'Once' (a coveted vinyl 78 rpm record of which was in our family collection on the yellow MGM label, sung by Billy Eckstine). This was a film that raised itself above its B-film status mainly due to Quinn's acting and the intriguing storyline.

RARITY RATING: 4/5
Only hope of release lies in the pressure brought to bear by film noir aficionados. Watch this shadow.

Anthony Quinn: No one went to sleep when Quinn was on the screen. His fiery temperament and pulsating passion were attributed to a bloodline that was a rich cocktail of Irish/Mexican. His high-octane personality made him a perfect choice for producers when casting a bullfighter (*Blood and Sand*), a Mexican (*Viva Zapata*), a Spanish painter (*Lust for Life*), an Eskimo (*The Savage Innocents*), or a Greek (*Zorba the Greek*). But the actor who gave the cinema these memorable ethnic characters started out life with a speech impediment that would have halted any advance as an actor had it not been for the corrective surgery that he had when he was 12.

Later Quinn answered an advertisement by Paramount Pictures in a newspaper stating that they were looking for Indians to act in the latest film by Cecil B DeMille, called *The Plainsman*. At the audition DeMille asked the young Quinn if he was an Indian and Quinn replied that he was a Blackfoot. He got the part and then eventually had to break away from the studio because he was being typecast. In over 160 films he played everything from a soldier to a bandit, from Mickey Spillane's hero in *The Long Wait*, to *Attila the Hun*, but he reached gold when he played Zorba, and again when he was cast by Federico Fellini as Zampano the circus strongman in *La Strada*.

He was passionate about the craft of acting and once likened it to boxing and bullfighting: 'It's a matter of adjusting to the other man's blows.'

See: *Larceny Inc.*

Windfall in Athens   1954

Directed by: Michael Cacoyannis
Written by: Michael Cacoyannis
Cast: Ellie Lambeti (Mina), Giorgos Pappas (Pavlos).

Story: Mina (Lambetti) buys a lottery ticket, which is then stolen. She gets a lawyer on the case and finds that it has been given to a vagrant named Alexis (Dimitris Horn). When the ticket comes up and Alexis wins, Mina takes him to court and wins the case, but then she falls in love with Alexis.

This is a charming little film that marked the debut of Cacoyannis, who went on to direct *Zorba the Greek*, starring Anthony Quinn as the eponymous hero, and the documentary *Attilas '74*. The film was nominated for best film at the Cannes Film Festival during its year of release.

RARITY RATING: 3/5
A film that Criterion should consider releasing in a new print on DVD.

Michael Cacoyannis: A Cypriot-born director who originally came to London to study law and changed career direction to become a film-maker, Cacoyannis gained media attention with his first film *Windfall in Athens*. His next two films, *Stella* and *A Girl in Black*, were equally successful on the European cinema circuit, but it was really *Zorba the Greek* that brought him international recognition. However, ten years after *Zorba*, Cacoyannis travelled from London to Cyprus to document the invasion of the island by Turkey leading to thousands of deaths. The filmed result was the brilliant, emotive documentary *Attilas '74 The Rape of Cyprus*, undoubtedly one of the great classics of our time.

The Light Across the Street   1955

Directed by: Georges Lacombe
Written by: Jean-Claude Aurel (play). Louis Chavance.
Cast: Raymond Pellegrin (Georges Marceau), Roger Pigaut (Pietri), Brigitte Bardot (Olivia Marceau), Claude Romain (Barbette).

Story: A lorry driver, Georges Marceau (Pellegrin), is involved in an accident and a doctor diagnoses that he should abstain from any sexual activity, but he marries Olivia (Bardot) and becomes extremely jealous and angry, and turns to murder.

Really a vehicle to project the 'sex kitten' Brigitte Bardot onto the world, it succeeded admirably because she became a household name synonymous with a certain kind of sexuality. France's answer to Monroe, she never quite got the roles that stretched her acting abilities and often appeared in lightweight comedies or inane features orchestrated by mentors like Roger Vadim, though the latter did give her a strong part in *Le Mépris* with Jack Palance. Most of her films are instantly forgettable but rising above the dross are *And God Created Woman* and *La Vérité*, in which France's master of suspense Henri-Georges Clouzot (*Wages of Fear/The Fiends*) directed her in her finest performance.

RARITY RATING: 4/5
One to be re-discovered and worth waiting for.

Brigitte Bardot: The 'Sex Kitten', as she soon became known the world over because of her amazing sex appeal, started modelling at the age of 15 and soon found herself on the cover of *Elle* magazine and later numerous film magazines when her film career was launched in 1952 with *The Lighthouse-Keeper's Daughter*. She pouted and posed through 44 more films from the early 1950s to the early 1970s. What you saw on the screen was Bardot playing Bardot, nothing more, nothing less, and that's all you ever expected. She smouldered in *The Light Across the Street*, sizzled in *And God Created Woman*, teased in *Babette Goes To War*, and was stretched to her acting limits in Henri-Georges Clouzot's *La Vérité*. It now seems incredible that any of her films might be lost to posterity.

Six Bridges to Cross   1955

Directed by: Joseph Pevney
Written by: Sydney Boehm. Joseph F Dineen (story).
Cast: Tony Curtis (Jerry Florea), George Nader (Edward Gallagher), Julie Adams (Ellen Gallagher), Jay C Flippen (Vincent Concannon).

Story: Jerry Florea (Curtis) masterminds an armoured car robbery, but in the heist gets shot by rookie cop Ed Gallagher (Nader). Gallagher tells Florea that he will never have children. Strangely they develop a bond of friendship and Gallagher gets promotion in the force. After a series of events and jail sentences, the friendship between them becomes strained as reform for the young hoodlum seems unlikely. Can Florea redeem himself to save his own skin?

I have fond memories of showing this movie as a projectionist and revelling in the charismatic quality of Tony Curtis. This is a well-above-average movie and deserves to be recognised as such. Sammy Davis Junior, who was involved in a car accident on his way to the recording studio, sang the title song having lost an eye in the crash.

RARITY RATING: 3/5
Copies of the movie can be obtained on the web but quality is substandard.

Tony Curtis: Handsome, wiry, erratic and paranoid is how he once described himself, but whatever Tony Curtis was, he was never dull and has always laughed and enjoyed life. Hollywood treated their new box-office prospect as a glamour boy who would bring in the girls and Universal, who had him under contract, along with Rock Hudson and Jeff Chandler, exploited that. 'They gave me away as a prize once – a Win Tony Curtis for a Weekend competition. The woman who won was disappointed. She'd hoped for the second prize – a new stove.' His keen sense of humour helped him survive Hollywood's hothouse for over 60 years, from his first feature, a low-budget comedy called *How to Smuggle a Hernia Across the Border*, to his latest, at the age of 82, *David and Fatima*, in which he plays a character named Mr Schwartz; Tony's real name is Bernard Schwartz.

In his early films, Curtis generally played a young hoodlum or a sabre-wielding Arab. Then he got the acting break he wanted when Universal cast him as *Houdini*. Suddenly he was recognised for his talent rather than his looks. The 1950s were good to Curtis and he reciprocated his good fortune by embracing the roles he was given: twice partnering Burt Lancaster, first as the opportunistic sycophant Sidney Falco, who attaches himself to JJ Hunsecker's side like a leech, in *Sweet Smell of Success*, and flying through the air with the greatest of ease in *Trapeze*. He took to the long boats with Kirk Douglas in *The Vikings*, chained himself to Sidney Poitier in *The Defiant Ones*, wriggled his hips and walked in high-heel shoes in *Some Like It Hot*, and ended the decade with the actor he impersonated in that film, Cary Grant, in *Operation Petticoat*. Yes, they were his vintage years.

When his career began to sag in the late 1960s, he reinvented himself by wearing a false nose and donning the persona of a notorious killer, Albert DeSalvo, in *The Boston Strangler*. It was the last of his really great roles.

See: *So This Is Paris*.

So This Is Paris

1955

Directed by: Richard Quine
Written by: Ray Buffum (story). Charles Hoffman (screenplay).
Cast: Tony Curtis (Joe Maxwell), Gloria DeHaven (Colette/Jane Mitchell),
Gene Nelson (Al Howard), Corinne Calvet (Suzanne Sorel).

Story: Three sailors, Joe, Al and Dave, played respectively by Curtis,
Nelson and Paul Gilbert, are on leave and head for Paris with only girls
in mind. They meet three, Colette, Suzanne and Yvonne, played by
DeHaven, Calvet and Mara Corday. They are all given a chance before
they leave the city to put on a show for a group of war orphans by singing, dancing and telling jokes for them.

Curtis gets a chance to sing and dance for the first and only time
in a musical, and does a pretty good job. Nelson, one of the greatest
dancers in movies, has ample opportunity to show off his prowess
and skills. Gilbert, on the other hand, is generally funny. They are
quite a talented trio and it really is a fun film, competently directed by
Richard Quine.

RARITY RATING: 4/5

Unless the musical genre becomes fashionable again, it is unlikely that
this lightweight but very enjoyable movie will be transferred to DVD.

Richard Quine: Started out as an actor but transferred to directing after having a job as an assistant director. Made some good if frothy
comedies during the 1950s featuring Jack Lemmon: *My Sister Eileen*,
Operation Mad Ball, *Bell, Book and Candle* and *It Happened to Jane*.
Though comedy was his forte, he occasionally surprised us with films
like the intriguing romance *Strangers When We Meet*, starring Kirk
Douglas and Kim Novak. But it was unfortunately his obsession with
producing the perfect comedy, which he was never given the chance
to do, that led him to his final act of committing suicide.

See: *Operation Mad Ball*.

The Toughest Man Alive 1955

Directed by: Sidney Salkow
Written by: Steve Fisher
Cast: Dane Clark (Lee Stevens), Lita Milan (Lida Velasco), Anthony Caruso (Pete Gore).

Story: A crime thriller involving an undercover agent, portrayed by Clark, who is sent to break up some Yankee gunrunners in South America. He infiltrates the gang and somehow survives until the last shoot out. The climax and ensuing carnage, located in docklands, is brutal and honest.

Clark never really climbed out of the B-picture pigeonhole that Hollywood placed him in but he always gave it his best shot. He had a distinctive and strong personality, not as sophisticated or as handsome as Alan Ladd or as dynamic as James Cagney, but he nevertheless acted taller than he was in reality. Often managed to portray tough guys with chips on their shoulders, cashing them in to always win the game in the end. The film's director, Sidney Salkow, ended up teaching film at the University of California.

RARITY RATING: 5/5
Sadly gone forever as no known prints survive.

Dane Clark: Despite co-starring with stars such as Bette Davis and Humphrey Bogart, Clark was mainly seen on television from the late 1940s onward. He felt much more comfortable in the role of the average guy on the street rather than a glamorous hero and average is what he attracted in the characters he played and films he made. He was proudest of the role of Abe Saperstein, founder of the Harlem Globetrotters, in *Go, Man, Go!* in 1954. There were other roles as a tough Joe Average in films like *Murder by Proxy* and *Thunder Pass*, but nothing spectacular, only ordinary fare. He once stated it this way: 'What I really get a kick out of is when cab drivers around New York lean out and yell 'Hi Brooklyn' when I walk by. They make me feel I'm putting it across OK when I try to be Joe Average.'

The Great Man   1956

Directed by: Jose Ferrer
Written by: Al Morgan
Cast: Jose Ferrer (Joe Harris), Dean Jagger (Philip Carleton), Keenan Wynn (Sid Moore), Julie London (Carol Larsen), Joanne Gilbert (Ginny), Ed Wynn (Paul Beaseley), Jim Backus (Nick Cellantano).

Story: No one has to read a TV prompter monitor to know that *The Great Man* is a great film if only the film could be seen. Ed Harris (Ferrer), a TV reporter, is given the assignment to present an hour-long programme to eulogise the famous radio icon, Herb Fuller, who was beloved by the nation and has just been killed in a car accident. He is told by the show's producer, Sid Moore (Keenan Wynn), that if he does a good job he will get better assignments. However, when Harris begins to question the people who knew 'the great man' he discovers that no one had a good word to say about him. He was a cruel, selfish, egotistical jerk. But Harris also finds that a lot of Fuller's cynicism and misuse of power has rubbed off on his co-workers. The dilemma that Harris faces is, does he tell the truth about Fuller or does he whitewash him for the sake of his fans and his TV bosses who expect a glowing tribute?

Al Morgan, who wrote page-turners such as *Cast of Characters*, *The Six-Eleven*, *To Sit on a Horse* and many other novels, adapted the film from his novel of the same name. Ferrer directs brilliantly and proves yet again what a great actor he was. The cast is excellent with Julie London – the blues singer and wife of actor Jack Webb – playing a very convincing Carol Larsen, a girl whose life was kept on hold for Fuller as his part-time mistress. But *The Great Man* also contains one of the greatest performances ever seen on the screen. No superlative could do justice to the acting of Ed Wynn (Paul Beasley) when he relates a story of Fuller, a man who was both a down-to-earth radio personality who people loved and a mean-spirited, drunken bastard who wrecked the radio station of the man who gave him his first chance in broadcasting. 'I know that some people find me ridiculous,' he tells Harris.

'Mr Beasley, I don't find you ridiculous at all,' Harris replies. Wynn did his six-minute monologue in one take and reportedly, after he finished it, the crew applauded and Jose Ferrer wept.

Like *Citizen Kane*, which was based on the life of William Hearst, *The Great Man* is thinly based on the real-life figure of Arthur Godfrey.

RARITY RATING: 4/5
Only source known for this movie is through Movielead. *The Shrike**
has since vanished, though a few video copies may be found on the eBay marketplace.

Jose Ferrer: Except for the role of Leopold in Woody Allen's *A Midsummer' Night's Sex Comedy*, there was a catastrophic drought in Ferrer's career both as an actor and director from the 1960s to the 1980s. Yet during the 1950s, Ferrer acted in some memorable films: as Cyrano in *Cyrano de Bergerac*, as Toulouse Lautrec in *Moulin Rouge*, as Lieutenant Barney Greenwald in *The Caine Mutiny*, and as Captain Alfred Dreyfus in *I Accuse*. But even these great acting roles pale in comparison to the brilliance of the two films that he directed and acted in, which now sadly seem lost forever.

* *The Shrike* was the first film that he directed, and he starred himself as Jim Downs, a man who is being committed to an insane asylum by his scheming, malicious wife, a part played by June Allyson, cast totally against character. The following year he completed a win double with *The Great Man*.

The Killer is Loose 1956

Directed by: Budd Boetticher
Written by: John Hawkins. Ward Hawkins.
Cast: Joseph Cotten (Det Sam Wagner), Rhonda Fleming (Lila Wagner), Wendell Corey (Leon Poole).

Story: Leon Poole (Corey) is a mild-mannered bank robber who escapes from prison seeking revenge on the cop who accidentally killed his wife, Detective Sam Wagner (Cotten). Sympathy mounts for the seemingly calm but frustrated Poole, nicknamed Foggy, because of his coke-bottle glasses. But soon we realise that Poole is a dangerous man, a psychopath obsessed with killing Wagner's family for revenge.

The outstanding thing about this film is Wendell Corey, whose ice-blue eyes are hidden behind thick spectacles, and who effectively conveys manner of a scary, mad killer.

RARITY RATING: 3/5
Bootleg copies of varying quality are available on the Internet.

Joseph Cotten: Starred in two of the greatest films of all time: *Citizen Kane* and *The Third Man*. Cotten's long association with his friend Orson Welles, and their early theatrical training at the Mercury Theatre in Ireland, helped him up the ladder to becoming a very successful actor. Hitchcock directed him twice: in the taut thriller *Shadow of a Doubt*, as the sinister Uncle Charlie, and then as Sam Flusky in *Under Capricorn*. Other memorable roles were as Eugene in Welles' *The Magnificent Ambersons*, as Lieutenant Tony Willet in *Since You Went Away*, as Jesse McCanles in *Duel in the Sun*, and Eben Adams in *Portrait of Jennie*. Cotten's last great part was playing opposite Marilyn Monroe in *Niagara* as her husband, George Loomis, whom she is conspiring to kill. Succumbed to taking parts on the smaller screen when movie offers began to dry up.

The Burglar 1957

Directed by: Paul Wendkos
Written by: David Goodis
Cast: Dan Duryea (Nat Harbin), Jayne Mansfield (Gladden), Martha Vickers (Della).

Story: Opens impressively with a newsreel that shows a wealthy spiritualist's diamond necklace, which is now being targeted by Nat Harbin

Larceny, Inc. (1942). Directed by Lloyd Bacon. Shown from left: Edward G Robinson, Jane Wyman. Warner Bros. Pictures/Photofest.

Lost Angel (1943). Directed by Roy Rowland.
Shown from left: James Craig, Margaret O'Brien. MGM/Photofest.

The Upturned Glass (1947). Directed by Lawrence Huntington.
Shown from left: James Mason, Pamela Mason. Universal Pictures/Photofest.
Photographer: Cyril Stanborough.

Black Magic (1949). Directed by Gregory Ratoff, Orson Welles.
Shown: Orson Welles. United Artists/Photofest.

Appointment with Danger (1951). Directed by Lewis Allen. Shown: Alan Ladd.
Paramount Pictures/Photofest.

The Long Wait (1954). Directed by Victor Saville. Shown: Anthony Quinn. United Artists/Photofest.

The Great Man (1956). Directed by Jose Ferrer. Shown from left: Keenan Wynn, Jose Ferrer, Edward Platt. Universal Pictures/Photofest.

Middle of the Night
(1959). Directed by
Delbert Mann. Shown
from left: Kim Novak,
Fredric March. Columbia
Pictures/Photofest.

Blast of Silence (1961). Directed by Allen Baron. Shown: Allen Baron.
Universal Pictures/Photofest.

Too Late Blues (1961). Directed by John Cassavetes. Shown from left: Bobby Darin, Stella Stevens. Paramount Pictures/Photofest.

The Victors (1963). Directed by Carl Foreman. Shown second from left: George Hamilton; centre: Vince Edwards; second from right: James Mitchum; right: George Peppard. Columbia Pictures/Photofest.

Sweet November (1968). Directed by Robert Ellis Miller. Shown from left: Sandy Dennis, Anthony Newley. Warner Bros/Seven Arts/Photofest.

and his henchmen. Harbin is constantly on edge during the robbery and afterwards at the gang's hideout by the railroad tracks. He also feels responsible for Gladden (Mansfield), the daughter of a safebreaker who had originally taken him in. The climax, with a reverential homage to *The Lady from Shanghai*, is particularly exciting, played out on the boardwalks of Atlantic City with all its glitz, gaudiness and guffawing funhouses, full of mirrors reflecting hilarity and horror.

Originally screened as a B picture when first released, a second feature to a forgettable first. Though it contains scenes obviously lifted from other films noirs, it is still well made and gripping in content. Duryea, as usual, is good while Mansfield is adequate as his gangster's moll.

RARITY RATING: 4/5

Satellite channels provide the only hope of seeing this movie.

Dan Duryea: Famously remembered by film noir fans as the blackmailer in Fritz Lang's *The Woman in the Window* and as the art forger and leering lout in Lang's *Scarlet Street*.

Duryea was menacingly magnificent in his roles as a slimy villain and soon became typecast as the man you would suspect of any unsavoury deed the moment you saw him. He never became a star but was one of the best supporting players you could find. His presence in a film made it watchable. He debuted in *The Little Foxes* in 1941, and continued to rise to the challenge of greater roles. In *Winchester '73*, Duryea peaked with his performance as the gunslinger Waco Johnnie Dean, a man who was dangerously crossing the line from sanity to madness whenever his hand reached for his gun.

A Hatful of Rain 1957

Directed by: Fred Zinnemann
Written by: Michael V Gazzo
Cast: Don Murray (Johnny Pope), Eva Marie Saint (Celia Pope), Anthony Franciosa (Polo Pope), Lloyd Nolan (John Pope Senior).

Story: Johnny Pope is a Korean War veteran wreaking havoc on his family because of his addiction to morphine. His pregnant wife, Celia, believes he is having an affair and seems totally oblivious to his addiction. His father, John, transfers his love and allegiance to Johnny's younger brother Polo, failing to realise how desperately his eldest son needs his love and support. Johnny needs another fix but cannot afford to pay his drug dealer Mother (Henry Silva). John Senior wants the money back that he loaned to Polo, but unfortunately his brother took it to pay for his morphine. Johnny decides that he needs to tell the truth to his wife and to his father about his addiction.

Tony Franciosa is outstanding in his role as Polo and was nominated for an Oscar. The film is based on Michael Gazzo's play of the same name. Gazzo wrote the screenplay along with Alfred Hayes and an uncredited Carl Foreman, who had been blacklisted by Hollywood for having communist sympathies. The play had attracted many star performers when it opened at the Lyceum Theater in 1955. The cast included Ben Gazzara as Johnny, Shelley Winters as Celia, Frank Silvera as John Snr, and Tony Franciosa as Polo. The role of Johnny was eventually taken over by Steve McQueen. Michael Gazzo based his play on an idea he originally had about a jazz musician who drank too much, but later he changed it to drug addiction after reading an article on the subject in the New York Times.

RARITY RATING: 4/5

Not available on DVD or VHS.

Fred Zinnemann: Winning Oscars for Best Direction and Best Film for *From Here to Eternity* and *A Man for all Seasons*, Zinnemann was highly respected by his peers in the film industry. He directed Montgomery Clift, Marlon Brando, Rod Steiger and Meryl Streep in their first films: *The Search, The Men, Teresa* and *Julia*, respectively. His direction crossed all genres from the classic western *High Noon*, to the musical *Oklahoma*, the drama *The Nun's Story*, and the thriller *The Day of the Jackal*. Zinnemann was once asked by a young studio executive to list what he had done in his career, and reportedly answered: 'Sure. You first.' He always emphasised that a film should tell a good story and entertain. 'The three most important things about a film are the script, the script, the script.'

A Man is Ten Feet Tall   1957

Directed by: Martin Ritt
Written by: Robert Alan Aurthur
Cast: John Cassavetes (Axel Nordmann), Sidney Poitier (Tommy Tyler), Jack Warden (Charles Malik), Kathleen Maguire (Ellen Wilson).

Story: Axel (Cassavetes) is an army deserter who gets a job as a long-shoreman at the New York docks by giving 25% of his pay to the fore-man Malik (Warden). He befriends Tommy (Poitier), who takes him home to meet his wife, played by Ruby Dee. Back at work, Tommy runs foul of Malik; during a vicious fight Tommy is stabbed in the back with a hook. Axel is determined to avenge his friend's death, even though he knows the army authorities could catch him as a deserter. He tries to get witnesses to the killing but none of his co-workers will come forward. They are scared of Malik, and of losing their jobs. Ulti-mately, Axel takes on Malik in a fight to the death and kills him.

In the wake of Kazan's *On the Waterfront*, *A Man is Ten Feet Tall* has been unjustly treated, because it is the better of the two films. It is so realistic due to the life-like performances of its leading players. Martin Ritt, who went on to direct Paul Newman in *Hud*, brings out the very best in his actors. Just observe the scene where Tommy is listening to Axel tell of his brother's death and deserting the army. The camera lingers awhile on Poitier's face, deep in concentration. It is a moment of intense sensitivity.

RARITY RATING: 4/5
Sometimes crops up on Turner's Classic Movies Channel, but other-wise unlikely to be shipped to anyone's home as a DVD.

John Cassavetes: Recognised as the father of independent film, John Cassavetes has probably inspired more filmmakers than any other director who has lived. His legacy is not only in the films he made but in those lives he has touched and influenced personally, his family and his loyal friends. Married to actress Gena Rowlands for over 30 years until his death in 1989 from cirrhosis of the liver, he fathered three children: Nick, Xan and Zoe, who have all followed their parents successfully into the film business. Cassavetes' friends Ben Gazzara, Peter Falk, Peter Bogdanovich and Seymour Cassell have appeared in his films on numerous occasions.

At the age of 22, Cassavetes appeared in his first film *Fourteen Hours* in a tiny uncredited role, which he followed a couple of years later with another bit part in *Taxi*. He bided his time while waiting for his next screen role by working in television, but didn't have to wait too long and was offered the part of Robert Batsford, a hoodlum who with his gang terrorises a suburban family. The film was remade some years later as *The Desperate Hours*, starring Humphrey Bogart. In 1957 Martin Ritt cast him in *A Man is Ten Feet Tall* and his career as an actor was confirmed.

But he wanted more, and as the money came in from his acting work he began to envision directing his first film, *Shadows*, in 1959. All his films were financed this way and when the money ran out he would take more acting roles until he had enough to continue working on his own films again. He never relied on mainstream distribution but often rang theatre owners directly and persuaded them to show his films. Finance for his next directing project *Too Late Blues* came from his successful TV series *Johnny Staccato* and from acting in an episode of *Rawhide*. His films appeared to be improvised but in fact were tightly scripted. He had a great ear for dialogue and his experience of acting helped him work well with actors who were in the main friends he had worked with before. 'I think my background as an actor is the only thing that has helped me as a director. It certainly helps to be aware of an actor's problem or laziness, and I think being an actor is the only way a director can really know the contribution of an actor without years of experience behind him. So I'm grateful that I don't have to go through years of experience of being hurt by my temperament.'

He directed his wife Gena Rowlands in seven movies: *A Child is Waiting*, *Faces*, *Minnie and Moskowitz*, *A Woman Under the Influence*, *Opening Night*, *Gloria* and *Love Streams*. His friend Ben Gazzara, who appeared in five movies directed by John, said of him: 'He never lost faith in anyone, especially if he saw that the artist was still trying.' Peter Falk, another close friend, added this remark about John's originality: 'Cassavetes was the most fervent man I ever met, and he didn't have a copy-cat bone in his body.'

John's compassion was illustrated by his friend Peter Bogdanovich with this story of why Cassavetes had broken ties in a production company with Robert Altman. 'It seems that Altman's secretary, despondent over an affair that went badly, had tried to commit suicide, and Altman had subsequently fired her. John said that this so disturbed him that he essentially ended the business relationship, and then hired the young woman as an actress for *Faces*. This was Lynn Carlin and she received an Academy Award (Best Supporting Actress) nomination for her performance.'

A photograph of John Cassavetes appeared on a sheet of American 37-cent stamps commemorating American filmmaking on 25th February 2003, a fitting tribute to a great filmmaker.

See: *Too Late Blues*.

Operation Mad Ball   1957

Directed by: Richard Quine
Written by: Arthur Carter
Cast: Jack Lemmon (Private Hogan), Ernie Kovacs (Captain Paul Locke), Kathryn Grant (Lt Betty Bixby). Arthur O'Connell (Col Rousch).

Story: Private Hogan (Lemmon) faces a dilemma when he meets nurse lieutenant Betty Bixby (Grant) because the army rules state that privates cannot fraternise with a superior officer; not only is Bixby an officer, but she's beautiful. If he wants to get to know her and she's not interested, it's familiarity with a superior. If she wants to acquaint herself with him and he's not interested, then it's mutiny and refusal to obey an order. When Hogan picks up Betty's cigarette lighter, he thinks he has a good excuse to speak with her, but he is spotted by security officer Paul Locke (Kovacs), who wants to have him court-martialed or even executed. Hogan knows that he can outsmart him and outtalks his superiors. Locke transfers Hogan to the mortuary, but he decides to hold a ball and finds a suitable venue. He schemes to win over Betty, but she discovers that he has tricked her with his X–rays to win her sympathy.

Great comedy pre-dating Altman's *Mash*, but definitely equally hilarious due to Lemmon and Kovacs. The latter sadly had a short-lived career, which fatally ended in an automobile accident. He was that rare individual who had original talent. Lemmon, of course, was weaned on comedy and explored every way to execute the right gesture, facial expression and body movement, to deliver a line with perfect timing and on cue. Another Quine direction that is infuriatingly lost.

RARITY RATING: 4/5
Operation Mad Ball could surface on TV courtesy of TCM, but maybe not.

Jack Lemmon: 'It's magic time,' was how Lemmon greeted each take before the camera, and, indeed, for thousands of moviegoers the world over, it was magic time when Jack was in a picture. He emitted an effervescence that was contagious in comedy and could also out-act many of his contempories in the darkest dramas. Always the consummate professional in 58 films, he often partnered his friend Walter Matthau and with him made ten films starting with *The Fortune Cookie* and ending with the sequel to *The Odd Couple*, the original version being their most popular.

The film that is considered one of the funniest movies Jack Lemmon ever made was his cross-dressing role in Billy Wilder's comedy

Some Like It Hot; his character Jerry/Dorothy was voted the 29th greatest movie character of all time by *Premiere Magazine*.

As a dramatic actor he challenged himself every time but his performances in *Days of Wine and Roses* with Lee Remick as an alcoholic couple, as Harry Stoner in *Save the Tiger*, and as Shelley Levine in *Glengarry Glen Ross* will be in the Hall of Fame as extraordinary and unsurpassed. But despite these great performances as an actor, Jack will be remembered mainly as the man who spread a little sunshine.

The Rising of the Moon   1957

Directed by: John Ford
Written by: Lady Augusta Gregory. Michael J McHugh (story).
Cast: Tyrone Power (Introduced by), Maureen Connell (Mary Ann McMahon).

Story: The film comprises three short stories each narrated by Tyrone Power. *The Majesty of the Law* is about an Irish smallholder and his encounter with the Law. Noel Purcell plays the farmer. The second story is called *A Minute's Wait*, another story of rural Ireland concerning the Ballyscran to Dunfail train and its one-minute stop. It is very funny and looks at the Irish attitude to time, which is the complete opposite to the Swiss one. Jimmy O'Dea is the lead in this tale. The final episode is called *1921* and is adapted from Lady Augusta Gregory's play *The Rising of the Moon*. It stars Ward Bond and is about the paramilitary force the 'Black and Tans'.

As is often the case with episodic films, one generally rises above the others in quality and in this case it is definitely *A Minute's Wait*, which is hilarious. Jimmy O'Dea sends up the Irish phrases that one generally uses when impersonating an Irishman. There is a wonderful side-splitting scene when there is confusion over bishops. The whole film is really a hymn to Ireland made by a man who had the emerald green running through his veins instead of the natural red stuff.

RARITY RATING: 5/5

It will take more than a kiss of the blarney stone to get this released.

Maureen Connell: Born in Africa, Maureen Connell never quite reached the top of her profession and her name was generally way down the cast list in a minor role. Her greatest success was starring opposite Tyrone Power in *The Rising of the Moon*. The following year she made *The Abominable Snowman*, playing Peter Cushing's wife, but after that her career declined and never picked up again. She married the director John Guillermin who directed her in *I Was Monty's Double*, which starred John Mills; again, it was another small part.

Wild is the Wind 1957

Directed by: George Cukor
Written by: Arnold Schulman
Cast: Anna Magnani (Gioia), Anthony Quinn (Gino), Anthony Franciosa (Bene).

Story: Gino (Quinn) loses his wife Rosa, and her sister Gioia (Magnani) comes to stay. Gino tries to mould her into Rosa in every way. Gioia is alienated by his behaviour towards her and rebels by having an affair with his son Bene (Franciosa).

Johnny Mathis sang the title song over the opening credits and the film was nominated for three Oscars. In retrospect *Wild is the Wind* is visually visceral because of the passion of its three leading players: Magnani, Quinn and Franciosa. Their verbal exchanges and emotive outbursts ignite every scene they are in. The tempestuous trio were three of the finest actors and Cukor wrung every drop of talent from them here.

RARITY RATING: 4/5

Unfortunately still not available on DVD.

Anna Magnani: Magnani allegedly said when woken by a reporter telling her that she had won an Oscar for Best Actress for *The Rose*

Tattoo, 'If this is a joke, I'll kill you!' Of course it wasn't a joke, the fiery Italian actress had won the coveted statuette. The part that warranted the award was that of Serafina Delle Rose, originally written for her by Tennessee Williams for his play, though Magnani never played the role on the stage because her English at the time wasn't good enough and the part went to Maureen Stapleton. It had been a long road to stardom, and while Al Jolson was wowing audiences in *The Jazz Singer* in 1928, the young Anna Magnani was at home in Italy making her first film *Scampola*. It would be 17 years before she appeared as Pina in Roberto Rossellini's *Rome, Open City*. The highly acclaimed film gained her international attention but still not enough to woo her to Hollywood; that would take another ten years, aided by the friendship of Tennessee Williams, who said of her: 'I never saw a more beautiful woman, enormous eyes, skin the colour of Devonshire cream.'

She appeared in three other American films, one of which was based on Williams' play *Orpheus Descending*, and was filmed as *The Fugitive Kind* with Magnani starring with Marlon Brando. Her last screen role was in *Fellini's Roma* in which she played herself.

The Philosopher's Stone 1958

Directed by: Satyajit Ray
Written by: Rajshekhar Basu
Cast: Tulsi Chakraborty (Paresh Chandra Dutta), Ranibala (Giribala Dutta).

Story: In this likeable but rarely seen comedy, a Bengali clerk named Paresh finds a magical stone that changes iron into gold by just touching it. The film evokes the fantasies of becoming suddenly rich. In the West, the dream is to win the lottery; in the East it is to find a philosopher's stone. The only problem that haunts Paresh (Chakraborty) is to find enough iron.

Ray, the cinematic genius of *The Apu Trilogy*, here takes to comedy with the same faultless approach. The acting is excellent and Chakraborty is a natural comedian. *The Philosopher's Stone* is a light-hearted story about a magical experience that is magically made by a master.

RARITY RATING: 4/5

May surprisingly appear one day at a Ray retrospective.

Satyajit Ray: Master of his art, Ray claimed worldwide recognition of his genius with *The Apu Trilogy: Pather Panchali, Aparajito* and *Apur Sansar*. Each film, and each frame of each film, was lyrically composed and poetically charged. Yet there's a simplicity about the scenes that are unforgettable. Whether it's watching a steam train on the horizon, a drop of water dripping from a ceiling, a spider falling into a glass of wine, a wide-eyed boy searching an old man's face, or pages of manuscript blowing in the wind. Whatever the images, they spelt out R-A-Y. His last big international success on the art cinema circuit was *The Chess Players* in 1977, but by that time he had already made masterpieces such as *The Goddess, The Lonely Wife*, and one, which has amazingly been lost: *Days of Nights in the Forest*; many of his films were based on stories by the great Indian poet Rabinath Tagore.

Fellow cinematic poet and Japanese movie master, Akira Kurosawa, paid Ray this compliment: 'To have not seen the films of Ray is to have lived in the world without ever having seen the moon and the sun.' Ray stood tall at six foot, five inches; and as a cinema icon he was a giant.

Wind Across the Everglades   1958

Directed by: Budd Schulberg*
Written by: Budd Schulberg
Cast: Burl Ives (Cottonmouth), Christopher Plummer (Walt Murdock), Chana Eden (Naomi), Gypsy Rose Lee (Mrs Bradford).

Story: An agent of the Audubon Society, Walt Murdock struggles to halt the slaughter of Florida's plume birds, whose feathers are highly prized for women's hats, and battles with the leader of the bird-hunters, a wild character called Cottonmouth. There is some spectacular photography of Louisiana's Everglades and shots of egret and wildfowl.

Definitely not the run-of-the-mill feature from Hollywood, this one. It has a motley crowd from all branches of entertainment to make up the supporting players: Gypsy Rose Lee as a farmer's wife, Tony Galento, a boxer, as a guy named Lout, circus clown Emmett Kelly as Bigamy Bob, writer MacKinlay Kantor as a judge, and Peter Falk, in his film debut, as a writer. The whole package is as colourful as the birds Murdock tries to save.

* Schulberg sacked the original director Nicholas Ray and reshot nearly all the material that he had made.

RARITY RATING: 5/5
Videos are now very hard to find of this film, but may appear on eBay.

Budd Schulberg: Schulberg was first and foremost a writer, and the son of BP Schulberg, the then head of Paramount Pictures. Notoriously famous for creating the ultimate Hollywood anti-hero Sammy Glick in his novel *What Makes Sammy Run?* in 1949, which caused him to be persona non grata in Hollywood for many years. There have been several attempts to make the book into a film, but so far nothing has materialised. In 1954 Schulberg wrote the screenplay based on his original story, *On the Waterfront*. The film went on to become a cinema classic and won Oscars for Best Film, Best Actor for Brando, Best Supporting Actress for Eva Marie Saint, Best Direction for Elia Kazan, and the Best Writer award for Schulberg. His next vehicle was for Humphrey Bogart, *The Harder They Fall*, based on his novel of the same name. *A Face in the Crowd* followed and then he took over from Nicholas Ray as director of his own screenplay *Wind Across the Everglades*.

Schulberg is still active as a screenwriter as his latest work, a documentary, is now in production called *Nuremberg – A Vision Restored*.

The Journey   1959

Directed by: Anatole Litvak
Written by: George Tabori

Cast: Yul Brynner (Major Surov), Deborah Kerr (Lady Diana Ashmore), Jason Robards (Paul Kedes), Robert Morley (Hugh Deverell).

Story: Caught up in the Hungarian uprising of 1956, a group of travellers are prevented from flying out of Budapest and put on a bus to Vienna. Before they reach the border, they are stopped and questioned by a Russian officer named Surov (Brynner). He believes that they are hiding a Hungarian freedom fighter among them, who they plan to take out of the country. A woman named Lady Ashmore (Kerr) is protecting an American passenger, Paul Fleming (Robards), to repay a debt that she owes him. Suddenly, Major Surov takes a romantic interest in Lady Ashmore.

Brynner is brilliant casting as the Russian and totally convincing. The film does have a tendency to lose its grip on the plot at times but is still worth seeing for Brynner alone. The film introduced Robards to the screen.

RARITY RATING: 4/5
Has never been released on DVD or VHS and is very unlikely to be.

Anatole Litvak: Russian-born director famous for shooting numerous takes of a scene. He came to the notice of Hollywood with the success of *The Amazing Dr Clitterhouse* and *Confessions of a Nazi Spy*, starring Edward G Robinson and Frances Lederer respectively. These two films firmly rooted him at Warner Bros studios. His highest point came when he directed three consecutive major hits for the studios in the late 1940s: *The Long Night* with Henry Fonda, *Sorry, Wrong Number* with Barbara Stanwyck, and *The Snake Pit* with Olivia De Havilland. His penultimate film before he died was *The Night of the Generals*, starring Peter O'Toole.

Middle of the Night 1959

Directed by: Delbert Mann
Written by: Paddy Chayefsky

Cast: Fredric March (Jerry Kingsley), Kim Novak (Betty Preisser), Lee Grant (Marilyn), Martin Balsam (Jack).

Story: Fredric March plays an ageing businessman and widower, Jerry Kingsley, who meets and falls in love with the young, beautiful and vulnerable Betty Preisser. She is constantly on edge, always afraid of what people and family are saying about her affair with Jerry. The barbed jibes are common: the age difference, she is after his money, and so on. In one scene, Jerry is on his own and feeling old with a blanket covering his legs and nervously twitching. Suddenly the phone rings and he knows it's Betty and his whole body begins to unwind and come alive. The scene is beautifully written and acted. Paddy Chayefsky was undoubtedly a gift to cinema with his fine adaptations of his own plays and his original material too, and one need only think of *Marty*, *The Bachelor Party*, *A Catered Affair* and now this gem of a movie. March and Novak are as compatible as coffee and cream.

RARITY RATING: 5/5
Lost in the dark.

Fredric March: March lived by his philosophy: 'Keep interested in others; keep interested in the wide and wonderful world. Then in a spiritual sense you will always be young.' That outlook on life saw him through over 50 years of acting on the big screen. During that time he picked up two Oscars for Best Actor for *Dr Jekyll and Mr Hyde* and *The Best Years of Our Lives*. His acting inspired younger men, like Marlon Brando, to act. He starred in the original *A Star is Born* with Janet Gaynor and played Arthur Miller's Willy Loman in the filmed version of his play *Death of a Salesman*. His love of his profession could always be seen in his great performances. 'There's so much mumbo-jumbo about acting. Spencer Tracy, one of the finest actors of our time, once told me, "I just learn my lines".'

Two of his greatest films have seemingly been lost: *Man on a Tightrope* and *Middle of the Night*. It is a shame that future generations will be denied further glimpses of this great actor's talent. Acting to Fredric

March was more than just a job. 'What I enjoy is working on a scene until I finally get it right. It's fun to know you're hitting it.' Metaphorically speaking, when it came to acting, March was a home-runner.

See: *Man on a Tightrope.*

THE 1960s

The decade when seven riders rode into town, when the word 'mulatto' became uncomfortable, even the moon mooned over Tiffanys, a couple of guys hustled over a pool table and it became a sweet life. A French tune about lovers kept whistling through our brain, Lancaster talked to canaries, Peck fought for rights from a classroom, Sellers had an urge to salute, Andrews danced over Swiss hills, Newman ate too many eggs, and Tracy and Hepburn's screen daughter had a surprise for them, while Ratso limped away as Nilsson sang: *Everybody's Talking At Me*. The 1960s were swinging all right, but some movies just never made it back to the dance floor.

The Sad Sack   1960

Directed by: Claude de Givray. François Truffaut
Written by: Claude de Givray. Andre Mouezy-Eon (play).
Cast: Christian de Tilliere (Jean Lerat de la Grinotiere), Ricet-Barrier (Joseph Vidauban).

Story: First and foremost this is a film to see not to talk about, but you won't be able to see it because, like other films in this book, it has vanished, so... Briefly it is a comedic episode about two friends who decide to take the mickey out of the army and their loathing of military service. Military service has probably ruined many a good mind but fortunately Truffaut used his experience to lash back creatively. Result: job well done.

RARITY RATING: 5/5

Even bootleggers have failed to tout this one.

François Truffaut: Nouvelle Vague was introduced to the cinema as a new way of making movies and it originated with Truffaut's *Les Quatre cents coups*. Truffaut tried telling stories in a different way using a lot of hand-held camera shots, freeze frame and improvisation, the latter employed beautifully in the scene where Jean-Pierre Leaud is being interviewed by a prison psychologist about his family life and sexual habits. Leaud was not informed of the questions before the scene was shot and had to come up with his own answers. The scene plays more naturally for it.

'When I saw *Citizen Kane* I was certain that never in my life had I loved a person the way I loved that film'; sentiments spoken by Truffaut that encapsulated his whole feelings about cinema. He was an infant when he saw his first movie and left school at 14. A year later he founded his own film club and met the French critic André Bazin who became his mentor. At the age of 21 he was a film critic for *Cahiers du Cinema*, the influential film magazine. Soon he was to become one of the most inspired filmmakers of his generation and throughout his career his love affair with film never ceased. No film has captured that love more than *Day For Night*, a film about the magic of moviemaking with Truffaut playing the role of a film director making a film called *Meet Pamela* with Leaud, Jean-Pierre Aumont and Jacqueline Bisset.

Initially Truffaut was a film buff who became a film director, actor, writer and producer of his own films, many of which were memorable: *A Bout de Souffle*, *Tirez sur le Pianiste*, *Jules & Jim* and *La Peau Douce*. 'I make films that I would like to have seen when I was a young man,' he once said.

Wake Me When It's Over   1960

Directed by: Mervyn LeRoy
Written by: Richard L Breen. Howard Singer (novel).

Cast: Ernie Kovacs (Capt Charlie Stark), Dick Shawn (Gus Brubaker), Margo Moore (Lt Nora McKay), Jack Warden (Doc Dave Farrington).

Story: Comedy in the Bilko mode. Gus Brubaker (Dick Shawn) is a GI who somehow gets himself entangled in bureaucratic red tape and finds himself being called up for the second time and having a second serial number. He is ordered to serve on an island off the coast of Japan under a hotshot pilot and commander Captain Stark (Kovacs).

LeRoy would not normally be associated with comedy but helms this one admirably like a true master of the genre. Kovacs is once again effortlessly funny while Dick Shawn emerges as a likeable newcomer who never really repeated his promise.

RARITY RATING: 5/5

Only ever seen on television, and recently, not even there.

Ernie Kovacs: Tragically the potential that this comedian had ended abruptly on 13 January 1962 when he was killed in a car accident. He made only nine films and was scheduled to play the character Melville Crump in *It's a Mad, Mad, Mad, Mad World*; Sid Caesar replaced him. Kovacs was hilariously funny in *Operation Mad Ball* and *Wake Me When It's Over*, both films which have since been lost. His comedy quips and antics came invariably as he chewed on a cigar à la George Burns, a unique but now sadly unseen talent, who preferred films to television. 'It's appropriate that television is considered a medium, since it's rare if it's ever well done.'

See: *Operation Mad Ball*.

Three Daughters   1961

Directed by: Satyajit Ray
Written by: Satyajit Ray. Rabindranath Tagore (story).
Cast: Chandana Bannerjee (Ratan), Nripati Chatterjee (Bishey).

Story: Three unrelated short stories from the master storyteller. *Post-master* is about a ten-year-old girl called Ratan. She is servant to a young man who is a poet, who's taken a job as the village postmaster in order to find inspiration for his creativity. The postmaster, Nandal, teaches the girl to read and write. Ratan was beaten by her last boss and is happy to find that Nandal is kind to her. When he contracts malaria, Ratan nurses him back to health. But soon, as Nandal recovers, he leaves to return to the city and Ratan is left feeling lonely and lost once again.

The third story is called *The Conclusion* and stars Soumitra Chatter-jee who was the leading actor in Ray's *The World of Apu*. A tomboyish crazy girl called Pagli attracts the attention of a young college student, Amulya, who chooses against his mother's wishes to marry the girl.

There were originally three stories, but the middle segment, *Moni-hara*, was never released due to budget restrictions and the inability to complete subtitling for the international market.

RARITY RATING: 5/5
Unseen in its entirety and likely to remain so.

The Colossus of Rhodes   1961

Directed by: Sergio Leone
Written by: Luciano Chitarrini. Ennio De Concini.
Cast: Rory Calhoun (Darios), Lea Massari (Diala), Georges Marchal (Pe-liocles).

Story: A Greek historical epic's account of an army captain named Dar-ios (Calhoun) visiting his uncle in Rhodes in the year 280 BC. A statue of Colossus has been erected in Rhodes overlooking the harbour. It's a magnificent-looking sculpture but inside lies a fortress and torture chamber. After an unsuccessful attempt to assassinate King Xerxes, rebels ask Darios to report back to Greece about a secret alliance with Phoenicia that Rhodes plans to oppress the people by slavery. But Dari-os seems more interested in the daughter of the builder of the statue, a pretty girl named Diala (Massari). Darios wants to leave for Athens but is stopped by Thar who is planning to overthrow King Xerxes. When Darios can't leave he decides to side with the rebels and sail on their boat. He is captured to be executed, then freed when the rebels attack. Later Darios is led into a trap by Diala, but manages to escape to join the rebel camp. In the battle the rebels are slaughtered and the survivors blame Darios for the carnage. But Darios redeems himself by entering the Coliseum and informing the crowd of Thar's treason. Darius breaks into the Colossus to destroy it and release its prisoners. There is a huge battle and a climactic earthquake aids Darios's attempts.

This is Leone's first gargantuan film that preceded his magnificent spaghetti westerns. There are plenty of the fantastic visuals that hallmarked his later films, even if the acting is a little hammy and the words may be out of sync. Still, it's a fun ride. Calhoun probably wasn't a strong enough actor to lead this battle and one can only wonder what it would have looked like with a Douglas or Lancaster in the role of Darios. Dream on.

RARITY RATING: 4/5
It should be available as an example of the great director's start in movies, but at present there is no announcement that the film will be released to DVD.

Sergio Leone: The spaghetti western started with this man and, though he had many people who tried to emulate his style, really no one came close to making them like he did: scenes would slow down, action happened quickly and then there was silence. His movies were like a dance that often began with a waltz and ended with a quickstep. Visuals were panoramic one moment and huge close ups the next. He was a master of the mise-en-scène; just observe the opening of his masterpiece *Once Upon a Time in the West*, a sequence that ran for 12 minutes before the credits disappeared. It opens with three killers waiting at a railroad station for a train that will bring them a man named Harmonica. Originally he wanted to cast Clint Eastwood, Lee Van Cleef and Eli Wallach as the killers from the Dollar series of films, but, when he couldn't get them, he opted for Jack Elam, Woody Strode and Al Mulock. The sequence was electric with Harmonica, played beautifully and enigmatically by Charles Bronson, being introduced to the killers by the sound of the harmonica deadman's chord and the train acting as a screen wipe as it passes out of the station to reveal the menacing figure of Bronson. Slowly the tension builds up as Elam says to Bronson, 'Looks like you are shy of a horse,' to which Bronson replies: 'Looks like you have three two many.' Slowly spoken dialogue followed by fast firing guns. And of course there was Leone's collaboration with the music maestro, composer Ennio Morricone.

What the observant viewer was rewarded with when they saw a Leone movie was crafted perfection, visually, audibly and kinaesthetically. In the film world, where the word genius has so often been overused, Sergio Leone was undoubtedly that – a genius.

His last planned project was a film about the siege of Leningrad during World War Two, but unfortunately he died of a heart attack two days before he was to leave for America to sign the contracts.

Too Late Blues   1961

Directed by: John Cassavetes
Written by: Richard Carr. John Cassavetes.
Cast: Bobby Darin (Ghost Wakefield), Stella Stevens (Jess Polanski), Everett Chambers (Benny Flowers), Nick Dennis (Nick).

Story: The spirit of the blues. Ghost (Darin) is a talented jazz pianist and his band refuses to compromise for the sake of commercialism and instead plays what they want to play – and that's jazz. But then love enters into his life in the form of pretty but neurotic Jess Polanski (Stevens), a singer. What is a man to do? Choose the girl or jazz? Ghost muses over his problem while accepting half-empty gigs in parks and old people's homes. There is some great jazz played with a soundtrack featuring Benny Carter, Red Mitchell and drummer Shelley Mann. Soon you get the feel of the mood of the movie and know it's a downtown downbeat as bluesy only as you might expect a Cassavetes signature tune would be.

Reminds me of the time I hung out at the Gaumont State Kilburn during the 1960s and saw a gig of gigs called Jazz at the Philharmonic featuring the Chico Hamilton Quintet, Dizzy Gillespie, Oscar Peterson and the Lady of Jazz herself, Ella Fitzgerald – all on the same bill. *Too Late Blues* never reaches those highs, but then Ghost isn't in their league. He is just a stubborn sonofabitch who is trying to play what he wants and isn't lucky enough for a record company to come along and lift him towards the bright lights. Bobby Darin was an extremely good singer who never managed to steal the spotlight away from Sinatra. In this movie you don't get to hear Darin sing but as an actor he was talented too. Stella Stevens was one of those actresses with charismatic promise but somehow it never happened for her. Like the title of one of Cassavetes' earlier works, they were shadows. Montgomery Clift was up for the part of Ghost but Cassavetes opted for Darin instead.

RARITY RATING: 5/5

Critics called it a *minor* work, while Cassavetes himself apparently was quoted as saying that it was his worst movie. It would be nice for us to judge for ourselves though.

Bobby Darin: The ultimate showman laced with a healthy dose of the charisma that kept Sinatra and Davis Junior in the spotlight for so long. Somehow his talent never transferred to the screen well, mainly due to the lacklustre acting roles he was given. There was but one exception and that was in *Captain Newman MD*, which got him an Oscar nomination. For a time he was married to Sandra Dee who was a fashionable starlet because of her success in films like *A Summer Place* and *Gidget*. Darin's screen success came from his songs which were used on the soundtracks of many films, the most popular being his version of the Charles Trenet hit *La Mer*, rewritten as *Beyond the Sea*, heard in *Diner, Sea of Love, Black Rain, Goodfellas, Havana, Apollo 13* and *A Life Less Ordinary*. In 2004 Kevin Spacey played Darin in the hit film *Beyond the Sea*.

Darin died in 1973 at the young age of 39 following open-heart surgery.

Freud   1962

Directed by: John Huston
Written by: Charles Kaufman. Wolfgang Reinhardt.
Cast: Montgomery Clift (Sigmund Freud), Susannah York (Cecily Koertner), Larry Parks (Dr Joseph Breuer), Susan Kohner (Martha Freud).

Story: Narrated by John Huston, his rich voice giving an authoritative and yet sombre tone to the subject he prefaces, *Freud* is a sincere and honest portrayal of the great psychologist. It focuses its attention on a case history of one of Freud's patients, Cecily Koertner, who has broken down mentally and physically after the death of her father. His method of treating her is to relate her neurosis to his own and by so doing not only cures her but formulates the Oedipus Complex theory – a child's fixation on the parent of the opposite sex. This is the whole crux of the film. It was Freud's discovery that there was not only a conscious state but also an unconscious one.

Here again was documented evidence that Clift was an amazing actor who because of his personal battles was born to play Sigmund Freud. Every moment he is on the screen you can feel his anxieties as if they were evaporating through the pores of his soul. As with most great actors, those who played opposite him were overshadowed by his excellence.

The dream sequences of the film were simply extraordinary and rate as some of the best ever filmed.

RARITY RATING: 4/5
Still waiting to come out of the closet and onto our video shelves.

Montgomery Clift: Monty was a brilliant actor on the screen and a disturbed one off of it. He carried his troubles inside of him but when he acted he was simply magnificent. His first ever role in *The Search* landed him an Oscar nomination, and three others followed for *A Place in the Sun*, *From Here to Eternity* and *Judgement in Nuremberg*. The part of Joe Bonaventure in Billy Wilder's *Sunset Boulevard* was originally written for Clift, and he was also wanted for the role of the sheriff in *High Noon*, but lost out to Gary Cooper. Clift brought a lot of psychological problems to the set, but these escalated after his car crash in the late 1950s resulting in facial disfigurement and severe concussion from which many say he never mentally recovered. Consequently, during the making of *Freud*, he was sued by the studio for losing production time due to his ill health. During the trial, it was announced by his defending counsellor that the film was a box-office success and the studio paid Clift a lucrative sum of money.

His last great screen performance can be seen in John Huston's *The Misfits*.

Kanchenjungha   1962

Directed by: Satyajit Ray
Written: Satyajit Ray
Cast: Chhabi Bishwas (Indranath Chaudhuri), Karuna Bannerjee (Labanya Roy Chaudhuri), Anil Chatterjee (Anil), Anubha Gupta (Anima).

Story: Kanchenjungha is the highest mountain peak in India and also part of the Himalayas. Chaudhuri and his family vacate to Darjeeling for their holidays and, inspired by Kanchenjungha, begin to reflect on their lives to each other in different ways. Anima confesses a love affair to her husband. Chaudhuri is worried at her husband's plan to give their daughter away in marriage to a materialistic man. While a young man named Ashok refuses to accept any job offer from Chaudhuri.

Yet another triumphant exposé of inner emotions by Ray that have been captured but unfortunately not released on film. *Kanchenjungha* is as visually poetic as the mountain it reveres.

RARITY RATING: 5/5

Convicts 4 1962

Directed by: Millard Kaufman
Written by: Millard Kaufman. John Resko (autobiography).
Cast: Ben Gazzara (John Resko), Sammy Davis Jr (Wino), Rod Steiger ('Tip-toes'), Ray Walston (Iggy), Stuart Whitman (Principal Keeper), Vincent Price (Carl Carmer).

Story: Based on the true story of John Resko who was convicted of murdering a man during an armed robbery in the 1930s. Resko was sentenced to the electric chair but Franklin D Roosevelt, then gover-nor of New York, commuted his sentence to life in prison only hours before he was to die. While in prison, Resko (Gazzara) learnt to paint. His art was recognised by a civilian instructor who took up his cause and he was released after serving 30 years.

Part of the film was shot in Folsom Prison with many prisoners taking part as extras, the rest filmed on a studio set in Los Angeles. The film was directed by Kaufman under the supervision of an edi-tor named Duane Harrison who had worked as Billy Wilder's editor on most of his films. Unfortunately he directed the film the way he wanted to cut it in the editing room and the film lost a lot of its sponta-neity and feeling as a result. There is a fine supporting cast headed by Sammy Davis Junior who wanted to really act and did so the way he performed on stage, with total dedication.

Gazzara tells a story about Sammy in his autobiography, *In The Mo-ment*, saying that he was utterly serious during the filming. However, he put on a one-man show for all the prisoners at Folsom at the re-quest of one of the governors.

RARITY RATING: 4/5
Still serving its sentence, the film has never even been released.

Ben Gazzara: I first saw Gazzara when I showed *End as a Man* in 1957 as a projectionist at a cinema in East London. It was his first film and he played the part of Jocko De Paris, a sadistic cadet at a military academy. His performance was electric and I knew that I was watching one of that rare breed of actors that would live on in my cinematic memory regardless of the quality of their material. Gazzara had a long association with his friend John Cassavetes and made some of his best films with him: *Husbands*, *The Killing of a Chinese Bookie*, *Opening Night*. Peter Bogdanovich was another director who worked rewardingly with Gazzara in *They All Laughed* and *Saint Jack*, the latter based on a book by Paul Theroux. Though the voice is now a little croakier, he is still acting, and was recently seen in one of the 18 visual vignettes that make up the delightful homage to Paris – *Paris, je t'aime*.

Something's Got to Give   1962

Directed by: George Cukor
Written by: Bella Spewack. Sam Spewack.
Cast: Marilyn Monroe (Ellen Wagstaff Arden), Dean Martin (Nicholas 'Nick' Arden), Cyd Charisse (Bianca Russell Arden).

Story: An intended remake of the Irene Dunne and Cary Grant 1940 comedy *My Favourite Wife*, famous for never being completed and for being Marilyn's last film. Nicholas Arden (Martin) is confronted with the return of his wife Ellen (Monroe), who he thought was long dead, on the very day that he gets remarried to his girlfriend Bianca (Charisse).

The film was eventually made with Doris Day and James Garner as *Move Over Darling*. Marilyn was dismissed from *Something's Got to Give* because of artistic differences with Cukor, who eventually rehired her because Martin would not work with anyone else. Unfortunately Marilyn died in August of 1962 and, though Lee Remick was sought to replace her, Martin's refusal halted the project.

RARITY RATING: 4/5
Though there is a 37-minute segment of the film, which is part of a

documentary made for TV and available on video, it does not include all the footage that was shot. The film will never be seen in its entirety because it was never completed.

Marilyn Monroe: So much has been written about her, much apocryphal, a lot sensationalised, and some just plain fictional. The truth according to her biographers and trusted friends is that there has never been anyone quite like Marilyn on screen or off of it. She was breathtakingly sexy and as photogenic as any cameraman could possibly wish for. She started out in small bit parts, many of which ended up on the cutting room floor. But she survived all of that, destined to be a star. Marilyn's magnetism is evidenced in everything from comedy to musicals, westerns to films noirs. One of her best-loved roles was that of Sugar Kane in Billy Wilder's *Some Like It Hot*. Her life, like her last film, was never completed, and plans for her to appear in the comedy musical *What a Way to Go* never materialised and the part went to Shirley MacLaine. She seemed to have had few loyal friends in her life, and most of her estate when she died was left to Lee Strasberg, founder of the Actor's Studio of Method Acting in New York, and Marilyn's mentor.

Sammy Going South   1963

Directed by: Alexander Mackendrick
Written by: Denis Cannan. WH Canaway (novel).
Cast: Edward G Robinson (Cocky Wainwright), Fergus McClelland (Sammy), Constance Cummings (Gloria van Imhoff), Harry H Corbett (Lem).

Story: Sammy (McClelland) is a child orphaned during an air raid in Egypt and is forced to live with a foster parent. Unhappy, he learns that he has an aunt living in South Africa and sets out to go there with only a toy compass for directions. The long trek is hazardous, the people he meets dangerous. There's a Syrian who tries to abduct him, a rich American tourist, and finally an old diamond smuggler named Cocky

Wainwright (Robinson), who becomes the boy's mentor until the old man is captured.

Quite a bit of the original film was cut before it was first theatrically screened, particularly the lustful sequence between the Syrian and the boy. The film was also beset with problems including two crew members who died of snake bites and Edward G Robinson who had a heart attack, but the film was made to rapturous acclaim.

RARITY RATING: 4/5
Was shown on Channel 4 a few years ago but still nothing on DVD or VHS.

Alexander Mackendrick: A director who could turn out a small picture about a fishing village, *The Magpie*, and then only a few years later direct Burt Lancaster and Tony Curtis in the powerful drama *Sweet Smell of Success*. Ironically, *Sweet Smell of Success* was a box-office and critical disaster when it was first released, yet the film about gossip columnists has since become recognised as the best film that Mackendrick directed. He came to film via directing and writing Ealing comedies, *Whisky Galore* being his first, and then he directed Alec Guinness in *The Man in the White Suit*. Some of his films have not aged well, but the delightful *Sammy Going South* is an exception, due to its young star Fergus McClelland and Mackendrick's adroitness in directing children. He had earlier coached a young Mandy Miller in playing a deaf mute in *Mandy*. The old film adage of not working with children was lost on Mackendrick who maintained that, 'Children are often better actors than adults, because they have a greater capacity for believing in a situation.'

Raven's End   1963

Directed by: Bo Widerberg
Written by: Bo Widerberg
Cast: Thommy Berggren (Anders), Emy Storm (His Mother), Keve Hjelm (His Father).

Story: Once again the genius of Widerberg is revealed in this remarkable film about a young man, Anders (Berggren), who is so disgusted about the vacuous lives that his neighbours are living that he writes a book about them. A publisher shows interest in the manuscript but is demeaning in his criticism of its author. Anders tries to find solace with his girlfriend Elsie (Christina Framback), which results in her pregnancy. Slowly the thought that his life is no longer his own makes Anders feel trapped and fearful that he is living a life as empty as his neighbours.

Thommy Berggren plays Anders and sails comfortably through the part, showing how well he and Widerberg understood and worked with each other. Berggren had the ability to immerse totally in a role and the sensitivity that allowed a moment's silence speak a thousand words. Like most of Widerberg's films, each frame offers a totally believable slice of life.

RARITY RATING: 4/5

The film has been seen at film festivals and often appears in retrospectives at the National Film Theatre, but has still not been released on DVD.

Thommy Berggren: Most of Berggren's best work was done with director Bo Widerberg: *The Pram*, *Raven's End*, *Love '65*, and Sweden's most successful film internationally – *Elvira Madigan*, a piece that plays like a beautiful concerto and looks like a Renoir painting. He played Sixten, a soldier who has deserted from the Swedish army to elope with a beautiful circus tightrope walker, Elvira Madigan, played by Pia Degermark. I saw this film at the Paris Pullman, Kensington when it was first released in 1967 and was totally mesmerised by the extraordinary performances of the actors. Berggren has always been at his best in Swedish films and on the rare occasion when he was wooed by Hollywood to appear in *The Adventurers*, his performance betrayed the weakness of an atrocious script and the film.

Berggren, like Widerberg, has lived in the shadow of Bergman's repertory of actors such as von Sydow and Bjornstrand, but can easily equal their status and often surpass it when he is given the right material and when directed by a cinematic genius like Widerberg.

Take Her, She's Mine   1963

Directed by: Henry Koster
Written by: Henry Ephron. Phoebe Ephron (play).
Cast: James Stewart (Frank Michaelson/Narrator), Sandra Dee (Mollie Michaelson), Audrey Meadows (Anne Michaelson), Robert Morley (Mr Pope-Jones).

Story: Frank Michaelson (Stewart) sends his daughter Mollie (Dee) off to college and is dismayed by her transformation into womanhood. He desperately tries to be the good father and at the same time stop her from getting into trouble, but without success. Soon Mollie has got herself expelled from college and flies to Paris and takes up with a French painter, Phillipe (Henri Bonnet). Eventually Mollie and Phillipe marry but not before her father embarrassingly falls into the Seine and gets arrested by the police.

This is a lighthearted film. Stewart comfortably glides through the whole affair, while Dee, fresh from success in *Gidget*, is adequately charming and adventurous. Includes a great scene when Stewart's costume falls apart.

RARITY RATING: 3/5
Appears on television, but it seems not even die-hard Sandra Dee fans can get a copy of the movie on DVD.

James Stewart: The 'aw shucks', stumbling delivery of words and the shy behaviour were some of the traits and mannerisms that endeared Jimmy Stewart to audiences over the years. He has probably made more feelgood films than any other actor in his time from *You Can't Take it With You* to *It's a Wonderful Life*, *The Shop Around the Corner* to *The Philadelphia Story*, *The Jackpot* to *The Glenn Miller Story*. But Stewart's range extended far beyond the romantic comedies of Capra and his ilk, as a bulk of his work saw him working under the direction of the master of suspense: Alfred Hitchcock. He suspected two killers in *Rope*, was encased in plaster and confined to a wheelchair in *Rear*

Window, chased a killer through a Moroccan market in *The Man Who Knew Too Much*, and was obsessed with the memory of a dead woman in *Vertigo*. And then there were his magnificent westerns such as *Winchester 73*, *The Man Who Shot Liberty Valance*, *The Man From Laramie* and *Cheyenne Autumn*. Stewart loved movies and thought that they just captured little bits of time.

The Victors   1963

Directed by: Carl Foreman
Written by: Carl Foreman. Alexander Baron (novel).
Cast: Vince Edwards (Baker), Albert Finney (Russian Soldier), George Hamilton (Trower), George Peppard (Cpl Chase), Melina Mercouri (Magda), Jeanne Moreau (French Woman).

Story: The story of a unit of GIs trekking through Europe in World War Two from Sicily to Berlin and the women they pick up, who serve as a relief from the horrors they have faced. Some of the soldiers will not survive and others will never forget what they have witnessed. The women, played by Melina Mercouri, Jeanne Moreau, Romy Schneider, Rosanna Schiaffino and Elke Sommer, barter their bodies and souls for cigarettes and food. Scenes are fired with the accuracy of a shell leaving shrapnel. Among all the bloodshed and loneliness of war there are moments of humanity like when Corporal Chase (Peppard) is on leave in England and waiting for a bus in the pouring rain. A working class family invite him into their home until the bus arrives. He is so exhausted that he falls asleep in an armchair in front of a roaring fire. When he gets on the bus, he realises that the family have placed a ten-shilling note in his top pocket. Another scene shows Baker (Edwards) stumbling upon some concentration camp prisoners escaping in the forest. One prisoner realises that Baker is not a German soldier and kneels in front of him and kisses his hand. And then there's the climactic scene that film aficionados have heard of even if they haven't seen the film: a soldier is executed for desertion by firing squad in a wintry landscape of snow while on the soundtrack plays the voice of Frank Sinatra singing *Have Yourself A Merry Little Christmas*. An irony as visually powerful as the soldier's hand reaching out to touch a butterfly in *All Quiet on the Western Front*.

A war film that ranks alongside *The Thin Red Line* and *Apocalypse Now*, *The Victors* is a masterpiece of filmmaking. Instead of being buried in a tomb it should be in a hall of fame.

RARITY RATING: 5/5
The film that was originally theatrically released in 1963 was quickly withdrawn and re-released in a shorter version. Both versions have not been seen or heard of again. It is unlikely that the original print still exists and a lot of footage is sadly gone forever.

Carl Foreman: First and foremost a screenwriter of immense talent who wrote some of Hollywood's finest scripts: *Home of the Brave*, *The Men*, *High Noon*, *Bridge on the River Kwai* and *The Victors*, which he also directed. His original screenplay for Marlon Brando's *The Wild One* was considered too controversial and subsequently turned down. Foreman was victimised by Hollywood during the 1950s for allegedly having communist sympathies, he was later vindicated, but not until after his death.

Terror in the City   1964

Directed by: Allen Baron
Written by: Allen Baron
Cast: Lee Grant (Suzy), Richard Bray (Brill), Michael Higgins (Carl), Robert Marsach (Paco), Robert Allen (Brill's Father), Sylvia Miles (Rose).

Story: A nine-year-old boy named Brill (Bray) is forced to leave home because his father can't afford to keep him, and hitches a ride to New York City. He meets up with Rick, a streetwise kid who controls the shoeshine and newspaper boys, and has cut himself in for half of their takings. He makes pals with a Puerto Rican kid, Marsach, and they start selling newspapers together. Brill then gets involved in a crap game with Rick and wins most of his money. Later that night Rick's gang set upon him but fortunately he's rescued by Suzy, a hooker. Next day Suzy takes Brill on a shopping spree for new clothes, then she's arrested by the police for soliciting. Brill takes what little money he has and buys a bicycle and heads back home but on the way becomes involved in an accident with a truck and his bike is ruined. An elderly couple give him temporary shelter before he finds his way back to his father.

Made on a very low budget this film still shows the talents of the man who made *Blast of Silence*. The film is rich in believable vignettes from an almost unknown cast. The film was also known as *Pie in the Sky*. When first released it was shown as a double feature.

RARITY RATING: 4/5
Appears on a website specialising in bootleg copies. DVD and VHS unavailable.

Lee Grant: Received an Oscar nomination for her first film role as a shoplifter in *Detective Story* and later won the award for *Shampoo*. Lee Grant often crops up in many films in character roles although she had the looks and personality to be a star. Stardom never came, however, and she often didn't fit the conventional roles assigned to her in films. She directed her talent mainly towards the theatre and television but is still quite something when she appears in films, even in a minor role in David Lynch's *Mulholland Drive*.

The Story of Asaya Klyachina   1966

Directed by: Andrei Konchalovsky
Written by: Yuri Klepikov
Cast: Iya Savvina (Asaya Klyachkina)

Story: Asaya Klyachina (Savvina) is a dancer who dances with the gypsies through Russia and tries to survive by her talent alone. She is passionate in her life and in her loves. She chooses her fate, her joys, her sadness, and finds her happiness no matter how fleeting.

Winner at the 1998 Berlin Film Festival, the film was made a year before the director's *A Nest of Gentlefolk* but has all the hallmarks of the latter, bathing the viewers' eyes with a beautiful balm.

The Story of Asaya Klyachina certainly is a classic in the true sense of the word.

RARITY RATING: 5/5
Only hope of saving it from oblivion is if one of the art house video companies such as Tartan or Criterion release it to DVD.

Andrei Konchalovsky: Worked as a screenwriter for Andrei Tarkovsky before directing. Came to the attention of the West with his beautiful character study and visual delight *A Nest of Gentlefolk*. Encouraged to go to America by Jon Voight, whom he directed in *Runaway Train*. Konchalovsky made his mark in Russian films and a retrospective season of his work is long overdue as is the release of his lost masterpieces to DVD.

7 Women   1966

Directed by: John Ford
Written by: Janet Green. Nora Lofts (story).
Cast: Anne Bancroft (Dr Cartwright), Sue Lyon (Emma Clark), Margaret Leighton (Agatha Andrews), Flora Robson (Miss Binns), Mildred Dunnock (Jane Argent).

Story: A group of Christian women are trapped in their American mission house in a war-torn town in China, which is on the Mongolian border. They are virtual prisoners of the Mongol warlord Tunga Khan (Mike Mazurki). Dr Cartwright (Bancroft), a newcomer to the mission, upsets the spiritual tranquillity of the place with her atheism and opposing views to the mission leader, Agatha Andrews (Leighton), a sexually repressed, cold woman. Ultimately it is Cartwright's strength of character that saves her fellow prisoners from the savagery of their captors by offering herself to them as a sexual slave.

Unlike anything that John Ford had done before but is as powerful and direct as many of his trademark westerns. Based on a novel by Norah Lofts, the film was released as a second feature to *The Money Trap*. The film did not connect with an audience that categorised Ford pictures as westerns.

RARITY RATING: 4/5

Has a chance of being released for its curiosity value.

Anne Bancroft: A versatile actress who was comfortable in dramas like *The Miracle Worker*, which won her an Academy Award, and comedies such as *The Graduate*. Married to actor Mel Brooks, Anne Bancroft's name in the credits of a movie generally guaranteed that the film would be both watchable and thought provoking. She delivered dialogue in a way that would inspire any actress to act. One can just hear the sincerity in her words and the syntax behind them when one recalls her closing lines in the film *84 Charing Cross Road*, which reveal her love of books and writing: 'I love inscriptions on flyleafs and notes in margins. I like the comradely sense of turning pages someone else has turned and reading passages someone long gone has called my attention to.'

The Thief   1967

Directed by: Louis Malle
Written by: Jean-Claude Carriere. Georges Darien (novel).
Cast: Jean-Paul Belmondo (Georges Randal), Genevieve Bujold (Charlotte), Marie Dubois (Genevieve Delpiels), Julien Guiomar (L'abbeLa Margelle).

Story: Georges Randal (Belmondo), cheated out of his inheritance and thwarted in love, discovers he has a natural talent for being a thief and takes on the bourgeoisie one villa at a time. Living on the edge of respectability he shares his booty with some nefarious characters but refuses to make it a revolutionary underground movement. When a fellow thief is gunned down, Randal still continues with his profession.

An ideal comedy romp with lots of fun and laughs along the journey, and Belmondo milking every scene he is in. Another Malle film that proves his versatility.

RARITY RATING: 4/5
No logical reason why the laughter that this film evokes should be stifled.

Louis Malle: A thorough and measured film director who brought his style of filmmaking to Hollywood when he made *Pretty Baby* and *Atlantic City*. He had the ability to make us take another look at a particular actor and see them in a way we haven't seen them before; a beautiful example of this is star Burt Lancaster as an old man remembering when he was a bodyguard for racketeers, and giving a wonderfully touching and funny performance as the ex-gangster's runner. In *Pretty Baby*, Malle launched the career of Brooke Shields at the age of 12 playing a child raised and living in a brothel; unfortunately Shields was unable to match this performance in later roles.

Bye Bye Braverman   1968

Directed by: Sidney Lumet
Written by: Herbert Sargent. Wallace Markfield (novel).
Cast: George Segal (Monroe Rieff), Jack Warden (Barnet Weinstein), Joseph Wiseman (Felix Ottenstein), Sorrell Booke (Holly Levine).

Story: Leslie Braverman inconveniently drops dead without warning, thereby inflicting on his family and friends all sorts of burdensome problems – his funeral for one thing. Braverman's friends gather for his funeral, among them Monroe Rieff, a public relations officer, Barnet Weinstein, Holly Levine and Felix Ottenstein. They meet Braverman's bitchy wife, Inez, who seems earmarked for Monroe's bed. There is wonderful Jewish humour, which is always at its best when it is politically incorrect and aimed at itself. Alan King sends up every Jewish rabbi and Geoffrey Cambridge stereotypes cab drivers. One scene eavesdrops on Monroe talking to gravestones telling the dead what has happened since they've gone. Another humorous moment finds a woman at the wrong funeral.

Many critics seem to have missed the joke about this movie and its Jewishness. The funniest Jewish jokes have always been told by Jewish comedians, as the world's greatest have proved.

RARITY RATING: 5/5

Video companies obviously don't see the joke, denying thousands of people the opportunity to laugh at this golden classic comedy.

Sidney Lumet: Still making movies even though he's in his 80s, Lumet is small of stature but a giant among filmmakers, though sometimes overlooked by critics. His success came with his first direction *12 Angry Men*. A character study of individuals under pressure and beautifully acted by Henry Fonda, Lee J Cobb, Martin Balsam and so on, the film is a student's dream on how each shot is set up without ever once *crossing the line*; the characters are correctly positioned right to left, left to right, without ever crossing over and therefore losing credibility. It's difficult to maintain if a film has so many characters confined in a small space, but Lumet does it perfectly.

Over 30 years after making *12 Angry Men*, Sidney Lumet directed a minor masterpiece that has been strangely overlooked, but if remembered at all now it would be because of one actor's name that was attached to it – River Phoenix. The film was *Running on Empty*, forgotten but not lost, unlike *Bye Bye Braverman*.

Sweet November 1968

Directed by: Robert Ellis Miller
Written by: Herman Raucher
Cast: Sandy Dennis (Sara Deever), Anthony Newley (Charlie Blake), Theodore Bikel (Alonzo).

Story: Sara Deever, suffering from a seemingly incurable disease, takes a man into her apartment every month. She chooses the men carefully and prefers to have those that are insecure and emotionally challenged so that she can send them away happy and cured. But November comes, bringing Charlie Blake to her, and they fall in love. It is a short and bittersweet affair as Charlie learns that the love of his life is dying.

Charming and irresistible, *Sweet November* is a film once viewed never forgotten. Now, though, it is rarely seen. It was recently remade with Keanu Reeves and Charlize Theron with disastrous results. The original is perfect because of its fine direction and the chemistry between its co-stars. Dennis is totally believable as the kooky but lovable Sara, while Newley, who was one of the most talented and endearing of all British actors, surpasses all his achievements as Charlie and the film is a fitting epitaph to a great man. It has become a cult movie and a favourite of all those who have seen it.

RARITY RATING: 4/5

Was last seen on Channel 5 but now seems to have disappeared. Video companies should really resurrect this movie and satisfy a need for a good story and great acting. Monumentally memorable.

Sandy Dennis: Winning Best Supporting Actress for *Who's Afraid of Virginia Woolf?*, Sandy Dennis was a dramatic and comedy actress who held her own with some of the top names in the business. Her comedy prowess came to the fore when she partnered Jack Lemmon in *The Out of Towners*, and her dramatic qualities in Robert Altman's *Come Back to the Five and Dime, Jimmy Dean, Jimmy Dean*.

Adalen 31   1969

Directed by: Bo Widerberg
Written by: Bo Widerberg
Cast: Peter Schildt (Kjell Andersson), Kerstin Tidelius (Kjell's Mother), Roland Hedlund (Harald Andersson), Stefan Feierbach (Ake), Martin Widerberg (Martin).

Story: Based on a true story, it tells of a strike by saw-mill owners and workers in the small Swedish town of Sandviken in 1931. The government send in the military to quell the unrest, but due to the inexperience of the commanding officer, the order to fire is given and five of the workers are killed.

This is Bo Widerberg's documentary-like account of industrial action in Sweden in 1931. It is filmed with the same impressionist style as *Elvira Madigan*: each frame looks good enough to hang in a gallery. Another masterwork.

RARITY RATING: 5/5
Why is this film no longer being screened at film festivals? Or released on DVD?

Bo Widerberg: Few directors have matched Widerberg's genius as a filmmaker, yet strangely his work has often gone unnoticed or even unseen. Though his subject matters were sometimes quite bleak, he offered a realistic way of looking at Swedish life, using very little of Ingmar Bergman's symbolism. He was sometimes criticised for beautifying serious subjects, such as the industrial revolt in *Adalen 31* or the suicidal pact of the lovers in *Elvira Madigan*, but photographing them like Renoir paintings only emphasised the irony of the scenes.

Widerberg proved also that he could make taut and tight-scripted thrillers like *The Man on the Roof* and *The Man from Majorca*, alongside a touching, charming little film called *Stubby*, about a small boy's passion for soccer. Yet another film in Widerberg's oeuvre which has since vanished from all screens, small and large, is the film *Victoria*, based on Norwegian Knut Hamsun's novel about a miller's son who falls in love with a rich girl and tries to win her hand and ultimately and tragically loses her. It never achieved the success of *Elvira Madigan*, though it followed the same theme of tragic lovers.

THE 1970s

Cinemagoers were given an offer that they couldn't refuse, love meant not having to say you're sorry, Roy Scheider was telling Richard Dreyfuss that they needed a bigger boat, Duvall was loving the smell of napalm, Walken preferred roulette, Moore was scoring Derek, a rabbit was getting bright eyed, and a couple of robots walked the desert. Why it was almost enough for Sellers to switch off the television set. La-de-da-la-de-da. Despite all of this a Ray, Widerberg, Bergman, Rudolph and Nichetti went missing.

Days and Nights in the Forest   1970

Directed by: Satyajit Ray
Written by: Satyajit Ray. Sunil Gangopadhyay (novel).
Cast: Soumitra Chatterjee (Ashim), Subhendu Chatterjee (Sanjoy).

Story: Four young men vacate to the countryside and meet two respectable women. Each is different from the other yet an understated sexual chemistry develops between them. When the men finally depart one woman's life changes forever with a new awakening of what life can offer. The men too will never be the same, as their view of rural villagers is enhanced and their city arrogance squashed forever.

Poetically still and mesmerising, *Days and Nights in the Forest* is a hymn to human understanding, a song to the senses, a cinematic jewel. There is a magnificence about Ray's films and he has left us all with a lyrical legacy.

RARITY RATING: 4/5

This begs for Criterion or a specialised video company to take it on, particularly as the film has been screened at the National Film Theatre Ray retrospective.

Fools' Parade   1971

Directed by: Andrew V McLaglen
Written by: James Lee Barrett. Davis Grubb (novel).
Cast: James Stewart (Mattie Appleyard), George Kennedy (Doc Council), Anne Baxter (Cleo), Strother Martin (Lee Cottril), Kurt Russell (Johnny Jesus).

Story: Three convicts headed by Mattie Appleyard (Stewart) leave jail to start a new life with the help of Mattie's money that he's saved and Lee's ambition to open a grocery store. The convicts are hunted down by their ex-jailer, Doc Council (Kennedy), who wants to steal Mattie's money. In the village of Moundsville, West Virginia, the townsfolk thwart the chances of the trio of going straight. However, Mattie and his friends are befriended by Cleo (Baxter), madam of the local bordello.

Mattie's glass eye was called Tye and it was so uncomfortable to wear that Jimmy Stewart could only film for 20 minutes at a time before he had to remove it. There seems to be a ruling from the Anne Baxter estate blocking the film's release.

RARITY RATING: 5/5

Unless the above-mentioned ruling is lifted then this film will never be seen.

Andrew V McLaglen: Son of actor Victor McLaglen, and mainly a director of westerns, having learnt his craft on TV with *Have Gun Will Travel*, *Rawhide* and *Gunsmoke*. He had a lot of success helming pictures of Wayne and Stewart, such as *Chisum* and *Shenandoah*. But for his biggest box-office hit he had to get off his horse to direct the war pic *The Wild Geese* with Richard Burton and Roger Moore. He rode tall in the saddle at six foot seven.

Happy Birthday, Wanda June

Directed by: Mark Robson
Written by: Kurt Vonnegut Jr
Cast: Rod Steiger (Harold Ryan), Susannah York (Penelope Ryan), George Grizzard (Dr Norbert Woodley), Don Murray (Herb Shuttle).

Story: A frontiersman, Harold Ryan, returns to his family after seven years in the Amazon. Ryan's wife, Penelope, has been struggling through those absent years in raising their son, Paul (Steven Paul), and endeavouring to ward off the amorous attention of the local Doctor Woodley and vacuum-cleaner salesman Herb Shuttle. Ryan tries to take charge of his forgotten family by bullying them but finds that his wife is no longer the same person she was; now she has become an intellectual and her love for him has moved on.

The film is very stagey but the conflicts and acting, particularly that of Susannah York, are excellent. All the characters carry their traumas as if they are grenades, with the pin about to be pulled. Though Steiger's character is only an inch away from exploding, Harper, played by William Hickey, is primed and ready to detonate: he was the last person to offload his bombs on Hiroshima.

RARITY RATING: 4/5
Has been viewed on television, but Kurt Vonnegut's writings are rarely considered commercial enough for repeated DVD viewings.

Rod Steiger: Had a penchant for playing biographical roles – Al Capone, Mussolini, WC Fields, Napoleon – but turned down the chance of playing General Patten, which George C Scott took, winning an Academy Award. His explosive delivery enabled him to be noticed and no greater example of that would be as a movie producer in *The Big Knife*. He got the chance of acting with Brando in *On the Waterfront*, but in the famous scene with him in the taxicab, Brando wasn't there because he had to leave the set early to make an appointment with his psychiatrist. When the scene came, the film's director Elia Kazan took Brando's place, so that Steiger would have someone to direct his dialogue to.

Steiger went on to play some very interesting and contrasting parts: the serial killer in *No Way to Treat a Lady*, the persecuted Jewish shopkeeper in *The Pawnbroker*, and the bandit in Sergio Leone's *A Fistful of Dynamite*. And in Fred Zinnemann's *Oklahoma*, Steiger was offered the opportunity to sing in his role as Jud Fry.

Joe Hill

1971

Directed by: Bo Widerberg
Written by: Steve Hopkins. Richard Weber.
Cast: Thommy Berggren (Joe Hill), Anja Schmidt (Lucia), Kelvin Malave (Fox).

Story: Joe Hill, a Swedish immigrant and political activist, attempts to organise the poor through speeches and songs, and is eventually executed for murder on circumstantial evidence. When Joe writes his Last Will and Testament he states that he hopes that his ashes can be scattered to help some frail flower grow. There is a moment when Joe meets a girl and they eavesdrop outside the Metropolitan Opera House until the door opens one day and a tenor invites the girl inside. She becomes the tenor's mistress. Unrequited love, justified homicide?

A criticism often aired about Widerberg's films is that they look beautiful but the subject matter is dark and sad. The director has defended his aesthetic, saying that the exquisite imagery helps attract a wider audience to topics that they would not usually go and see. Berggren once again plays the protagonist.

RARITY RATING: 4/5
Some day all of Widerberg's films will be scattered like ashes, and help inspire future filmmakers. Alas, until then, this film lies buried.

A Safe Place

Directed by: Henry Jaglom
Written by: Henry Jaglom
Cast: Tuesday Weld (Susan/Noah), Orson Welles (Magician), Jack Nicholson (Mitch), Phil Proctor (Fred).

Story: A young woman from New York, Susan, is torn between the past and the present. The present offers her two lovers, Mitch (Nicholson) and Fred (Proctor), while the past offers a kindly and wise magician played by Welles. The film moves back and forth between fantasy and reality until Susan decides her fate.

A film shot in 41 days and Jaglom's directorial debut, it received poor distribution when released theatrically and practically caused a riot when screened at the New York Film Festival.

RARITY RATING: 5/5
For art house audiences and cinephiles, not the dilettante. Another prospect for Criterion's coveted library.

Henry Jaglom: Described by one film critic as 'the world's worst film director' and by actress Candice Bergen as 'confrontational'. His own brother said: 'I'm totally amazed he hasn't gotten beaten up.' Henry Jaglom raises temperatures off and on the screen. Temper wasn't only reserved for him personally but also for his films: Jaglom once stormed into a restaurant and accused a critic of hating *A Safe Place*. The astonished critic replied, 'But Henry, everybody hated your film.' What makes Jaglom interesting is the unconventional way in which his films are told and made, often on a shoestring budget. There is a story that Jack Nicholson once said to him that he would work for nothing as long as he was given a television set. Opponents of his work claim that his films are self-indulgent exercises. *Last Summer at the Hamptons*, a movie of sheer beauty, would be a defence.

In 1997 a documentary was made about the controversial director called *Who is Henry Jaglom?*

Four Nights of a Dreamer 1971

Directed by: Robert Bresson
Written by: Robert Bresson (screenplay).
Cast: Isabelle Weingarten (Marthe), Guillaume des Forets (Jacques), Maurice Monnoyer (Lover).

Story: Returning from a day in the country, Jacques (des Forets) stops a young girl, Marthe (Weingarten), from jumping off the Pont Neuf. After he takes her home they agree to meet the next day on the same bridge. She recounts to him that she tried to commit suicide because her lover promised to meet her and didn't show up. Jacques tries to find him for her but when he again fails to show she transfers her attention to Jacques who has fallen in love with her. But unfortunately for Jacques the lover eventually turns up and Marthe chooses him.

 Four Nights of a Dreamer is really a story of two lost dreamers meeting with their hearts rather than their heads. It reflects Bresson's themes of aimlessness, loneliness, reality and fantasies. There are some beautiful romantic settings, which are enforced by a wonderful Brazilian soundtrack.

RARITY RATING: 3/5
Although of poor quality, the film is available from pirated sources on the Internet.

Robert Bresson: 'For me, filmmaking is combining images and sounds of real things in an order that makes them effective. What I disapprove of is photographing things that are not real: sets and actors are not real.' Bresson's film philosophy led to a style that was very minimalist and bordered on documentary. He made only 14 films in his lifetime but his films are still quite rare in their quality and sincere belief that it's image that's important. One only has to think of *Jeanne d'Arc*, and the close ups of Falconetti, head tilted to one side, her face betraying her fate, are immediately conjured. One only has to hear the sound of tinkling bells to envision the sight of the wretched donkey in *Au hazard*

Balthazar. Considered by some as a genius and by others a bore, Bresson's films courted controversy.

Summertree   1971

Directed by: Anthony Newley
Written by: Stephen Yafa
Cast: Michael Douglas (Jerry), Jack Warden (Herb), Brenda Vaccaro (Venetta), Barbara Bel Geddes (Ruth).

Story: The subject is Vietnam and the arguments that ensue between Jerry and his diehard father Herb. Caught between their war of words is Venetta, who has divided loyalities, being Jerry's mother and Herb's wife. The privileged few that have seen this movie will remember the haunting soundtrack 'Having the Time of our Lives' featuring a guitar solo, and a remarkable acting performance by veteran actor William Smith who played a Draft Lawyer.

Kirk Douglas bought the play for his son Michael after he was fired from the stage production and his company Bryna produced the film. Douglas entrusted the direction of the film to Anthony Newley after having directed only one film, the very controversial and self-indulgent *Can Hieronymous Merkin Ever Forget Mercy Humppe and Find True Happiness?* In the cast of *Summertree* was another famous film director, Rob Reiner, who played the role of Don.

RARITY RATING: 5/5
Summertree is unseen and unheard of by the majority of filmgoers.

Michael Douglas: Early success came via the small screen with the hit cop series *Streets of San Francisco* and then he partnered Kathleen Turner in the adventurous and funny *Romancing the Stone*. In 1975, he produced the film *One Flew Over The Cuckoo's Nest*, which was a great success with Jack Nicholson in the lead. He has appeared in some interesting films, both lightweight comedy and edge-of-your-seat thrillers. During the 1990s he was cast against strong women:

Basic Instinct with Sharon Stone, *Fatal Attraction* with Glenn Close, and *Disclosure* with Demi Moore. Despite being only a minor hit at the box office, one of his enduring and endearing roles was that of Professor Grady Tripp in *Wonder Boys*. Son of veteran actor Kirk Douglas.

The Most Wonderful Evening of My Life   1972

Directed by: Ettore Scola
Written by: Ettore Scola. Friedrich Durrenmatt (play).
Cast: Alberto Sordi (Alfredo Rossi), Michel Simon (Attorney Zorn), Charles Vanel (Il Presidente), Claude Dauphin (Cancelliere Bouisson), Janet Agren (Simonetta).

Story: Three retired magistrates decide that they want to continue judging people and contemplate their victims in a mansion in Switzerland. Tired of the game of convicting historic figures long dead – Joan of Arc, Dreyfus and others – they turn their attention to the living. Alberto Rossi (Sordi) is a good candidate as he has a monstrous past.

The film plays like an Agatha Christie whodunit with lots of twists and unexpected laughs. Sordi is at his best.

RARITY RATING: 4/5
The whereabouts of this gem look likely to remain a mystery for a long time to come.

Ettore Scola: Collaborated with his daughter Silvia on the screenplays of many of his films. During the 1970s, Scola made two films that were visually exquisite: *We All Loved Each Other So Much* and *The Most Wonderful Evening of My Life*, the latter title having now been lost along with his visual hymn to cinema: *Splendor*.

The Friends of Eddie Coyle   1973

Directed by: Peter Yates
Written by: Paul Monash. George V Higgins (novel).

Cast: Robert Mitchum (Eddie Coyle), Peter Boyle (Dillon), Richard Jordan (Dave Foley), Steven Keats (Jackie Brown), Alex Rocco (Jimmy Scalise).

Story: Time is running out for Eddie Coyle (Mitchum), a two-bit hoodlum who is facing a two-year jail term and wants out. He does not want to see his wife and kids go on welfare, so tries to do a deal with the state's district attorney. Coyle has been hurt too many times and he doesn't intend to get hurt this time. He has his friends of course, but can he really rely on them?

Mitchum is excellent in this part and gives one of his greatest performances. All of Mitchum's trademark gestures and expressions are on display: droopy-eyed and laconic, monosyllabic mutterings, and dangerously menacing. Yates does a good job of directing and the film is finely tuned.

RARITY RATING: 3/5
Occasionally aired on TV but no release to DVD is imminent. There is a pirated copy available on the Internet of dubious quality.

Robert Mitchum: Droopy-eyed and lethargic in appearance, yet beneath that somnambulence was an extremely skilled actor who joked away his performances as easy, saying that he only made movies to get laid, smoke some pot, and make money. But Mitch was a professional in every sense of the word. His was nominated for an Oscar for *The Story of G.I. Joe* and took the most challenging of roles when he appeared in the Charles Laughton horror/thriller *The Night of the Hunter* playing the Satanic sex-obsessed preacher who mesmerises a woman and her children into his trust. The scenes involving the children were directed by Mitchum as Laughton hated working with them. The film was probably Mitchum's best role but unfortunately it struck disaster at the box office. Laughton, its director, was never allowed to direct another film again. He was also beautifully cast in the film noir story of *Build My Gallows High* as the man hired by gangster Kirk Douglas to find his girl Jane Greer.

The Midnight Man   1974

Directed by: Roland Kibbee. Burt Lancaster.
Written by: Roland Kibbee. David Anthony (novel).
Cast: Burt Lancaster (Jim Slade), Susan Clark (Linda Thorpe), Cameron Mitchell (Quartz).

Story: Jim Slade, an ex-homicide investigator, has just been released from prison for shooting his wife and her lover. He takes a night watchman's job at a college and when a murder is committed there he begins to investigate the crime. Local law enforcement officers hinder his progress and perilous obstacles are put in his path. But a skilled determination and an iron resolve to find the killer allow Slade to uncover a crime shrouded in deceit and corruption.

Good thriller with Lancaster on top form. He gets good support from Clark and Mitchell, and watch out for the young man playing the character of King: Burt Lancaster's son, Bill.

RARITY RATING: 3/5
Screened on TV a number of years ago but not released to DVD.

At Long Last Love   1975

Directed by: Peter Bogdanovich
Written by: Peter Bogdanovich
Cast: Burt Reynolds (Michael Pritchard), Cybill Shepherd (Brooke Carter), Madeline Kahn (Kitty O'Kelly).

Story: Michael Pritchard is a playboy sizing up the very beautiful heiress Brooke Carter. Paths cross with a Broadway star Kitty O'Kelly (Kahn) and an Italian gambler Johnny Spanish (Duillo Del Prete). There are plenty of excuses to break into song and display Cole Porter's prowess as a songwriter with *It's De-Lovely*, *Well, Did You Ever?* and

Just One of Those Things. Cybill Shepherd is very good and Reynolds is reminiscent of Clark Gable in *Idiot's Delight*.

The performances were actually sung on camera and the voices were not dubbed later as is the general practice.

RARITY RATING: 5/5
Bogdanovich owns the rights and has stated that he does intend to release the film on DVD.

Peter Bogdanovich: 'Remember me? I used to be Peter Bogdanovich,' was how he once introduced himself to producer Irwin Winkler. It was a period when he had fallen from grace in Hollywood, where studio executives only remember hits. But some directors cross the line in their careers from box office to art house, and in retrospect that was what happened to Bogdanovich. He came to critical attention when he made a low-budget 90-minute feature called *Targets* that starred Boris Karloff as an old horror star who makes a personal appearance at a drive-in theatre, and confronts a psychotic Vietnam veteran who has taken to the roof of a building with a telescopic rifle and is killing people at random. The movie theme was used later in the box-office hits *The Last Picture Show* and *What's Up, Doc? Nickelodeon* and *Texasville* took a nostalgic glance at movies too, but not with the same success. Directing Ryan O'Neal's daughter Tatum in *Paper Moon* led to her winning an Oscar for the film, and whilst *Saint Jack* and *They All Laughed* were critically applauded, producers weren't forthcoming with money.

During his youth, Bogdanovich was an obsessive moviegoer, seeing over 400 movies a year, and it was this passion for movies that led him to an unsurpassable knowledge of film, which he has tapped into frequently with the many superb books he has written on the subject: *The Cinema Series on Hitchcock*, *Hawks* and *Welles*; *Who the Devil Made It*, *Who The Hell's In It*, and the excellent *This is Orson Welles*.

Recently he launched a new Internet channel called *The Golden Age of Movies with Peter Bogdanovich*, offering his commentary and perspective on great cinema of the past.

Face to Face

Directed by: Ingmar Bergman
Written by: Ingmar Bergman
Cast: Liv Ullmann (Dr Jenny Isaksson), Erland Josephson (Dr Tomas Jacobi), Aino Taube (Grandmother), Gunnar Bjornstrand (Grandfather).

Story: Liv Ullmann portrays a psychiatrist, Dr Jenny Isaksson, suffering from mental illness and, on camera, we see self-treatment exposing every nerve, every fibre of her being in an attempt to cure herself. Her parents were cold and distant, her relationship with a fellow doctor too fleeting, the love for her daughter too painful. Between all of these are her demonic nightmares and dreams, each interchanging with one another until the dividing line is inseparable and she is unable to tell the difference between the two.

Probably no other actress could subject herself to such scrutiny as Ullmann, who is constantly on screen. Bergman gives her the clay and Ullmann shapes and moulds it to her persona. Sometimes the fantasy sequences get in the way and distract us from our journey into this woman's soul, but Ullman never compromises her stance, her direction, her obsessions: they are there for all to see. Like all Bergman films you feel as if you're lying on a couch being analysed and you expect him to question your feelings towards death and suicide. This is no exception, only we are with the patient and feel her pain and traumas. It does not make for easy viewing, only memorable acting.

RARITY RATING: 3/5
As yet unreleased on DVD, but it surely will be.

Ingmar Bergman: 'Theatre is the faithful wife. Film is the great adventure – the costly mistress.' And Bergman entertained his mistress by showing her in close up through symbolic images that take root in your mind; once seen they are never forgotten. The Swedish master filmmaker retired from his craft as a film director in 1984 after he made *Fanny and Alexander*, perhaps his most accessible and optimistic work, and transferred his attention to writing and directing for TV.

He was offered his first chance to direct when he replaced Alf Kjell-in on the film *Hets*, directing the last sequence. *Crisis* was his first feature film and told the story of an 18-year-old girl who gives piano lessons and lets a room to a man that loves her. Seeking a more exciting life she leaves with her mother for Stockholm. The film contained many of the hallmarks that would come to be recognised as Bergmanesque touches.

Two of his most significant works were *The Seventh Seal*, starring Max von Sydow and Gunnar Bjornstrand, and *Wild Strawberries*, with Victor Sjostrom. The former had the memorable sequence of a knight playing a game of chess with Death, while the latter chronicled an old college professor's journey into his past. Both films were filled with incredible symbolic images.

Ingmar Bergman died in 2007 aged 89.

We Can't Go Home Again   1976

Directed by: Nicholas Ray
Written by: Tom Farrell. Nicholas Ray.
Cast: Ritchie Block (Ritchie), Tom Farrell (Tom Farrell), Danny Fisher (Danny), Jill Gannon (Jill), Jane Heymann (Jane).

Story: Probably one of the most unconventional movies ever made with actors just improvising their lines in front of a series of projectors. There's little story and the whole thing seems a mess but Ray's acting students are acting their souls out for him.

Ray made two versions of this film and only the original remains, and that is never seen. It was made on a shoestring budget and Ray used a Mitchell camera that he said he bought from a surplus navy store.

RARITY RATING: 5/5
Unattainable and unobtainable, yet a glimpse of the film can be seen in Wim Wenders' documentary on Ray, *Lightning Over Water*, which was

directed by Ray and Wenders, the latter taking over when Ray could no longer direct due to cancer. The film becomes a record of a dying man.

Nicholas Ray: One of the few directors that quite honestly started a cult following, due to the youth that identified with his favourite themes of loners and people trying to find their place in society. His heroes and heroines were misfits and rebelled. There was Joan Crawford toting a gun in the classic western *Johnny Guitar*, James Dean as the crazy, mixed-up delinquent in *Rebel Without a Cause*, Anthony Quinn as the isolated Innuit in *The Savage Innocents*.

Ray's films were different, forceful and undoubtedly memorable. A massive heart attack while filming *55 Days at Peking* started a downward spiral of ill health, but like his heroes he was a fighter and still managed to make another three films, among which was the quite extraordinary feature *We Can't Go Home Again*. Among his many devotees were Jean-Luc Godard and Wim Wenders, but his personal life was tainted by the bad press that he received when his ex-wife Gloria Grahame married his son.

An Enemy of the People   1978

Directed by: George Schaefer
Written by: Alexander Jacobs. Henrik Ibsen (play).
Cast: Steve McQueen (Dr Thomas Stockmann), Bibi Andersson (Catherine Stockmann), Charles Durning (Peter Stockmann), Richard A Dysart (Aslaksen).

Story: Dr Thomas Stockmann (McQueen), a scientist, stands up against a town when he discovers that the water in the local spa is polluted. Feeling that the town's plan to open the spa should stop, he tells the town's mayor and also his brother, Peter (Durning). To Tom's amazement his brother refuses to stop the project saying that the costs would be enormous and potential tourists would be scared off. Tom takes his story to the owners of the local newspaper and they are willing to print the story, but then Peter informs them that printing the article would result in a large taxation rise to pay for the clean up, and that would be a vote loser. The paper withdraws the article and Tom's efforts to speak to the townsfolk are rejected; and he finds himself ostracised and an outcast.

The public image of McQueen was blown when the audience saw him as a hirsute scientist, which resulted in the film being withdrawn after poor box-office receipts. The film played on Pay TV in the late 70s and had its US TV premiere on SelectTV, which covered the Los Angeles area. In New York, the film screened at a few art houses in 1981.

RARITY RATING: 3/5
Was released by Warner Home Video and some of these copies appear occasionally on eBay.

Steve McQueen: Racing was his life, and his passion for the sport was exemplified in *The Great Escape*, *Le Mans* and of course *Bullitt*, in which he did his own stunts. But, ironically, it was the exposure to asbestos in the lining of his race suits and his habit of soaking rags in the substance to cover his mouth while racing that led to his death from cancer. Like the characters that he played on the screen, McQueen took great risks in a life that began in reform schools and had him pronounced dead twice from stomach cancer. He had a huge following of fans, playing the gunslinger in *The Magnificent Seven*, the lover in *The Thomas Crown Affair* and the escaped convict in *Papillon*. An actor once commented about McQueen's acting that 'he doesn't bring much to the party,' but maybe it was just because he burst too many partygoer's balloons.

Remember My Name   1978

Directed by: Alan Rudolph
Written by: Alan Rudolph
Cast: Geraldine Chaplin (Emily), Anthony Perkins (Neil).

Story: An unstable woman named Emily takes a boarding-house room in a small town for the purpose of stalking a man with the intent to kill him. Neil seems a little crazy too, but is no match for Emily who tosses stones at his window and rips up his flowerbeds. With such edgy people, violence feels only a breath away.

A Rudolph film that just begs to be seen. Chaplin adopts another curious accent but is still riveting in her quirkiness. Perkins gives one of his strongest performances to date and is far removed from the psychotic he was famous for playing in *Psycho*; here we see a gentleness and it is only because of our cinematic memories that we think he may be capable of darker deeds.

RARITY RATING: 4/5
Without A-list stars and a director whose name spells box office, this may never be transferred to DVD. A great shame.

Alan Rudolph: People often find it hard to name a Rudolph film and his work has never achieved the same recognition as that of his friend Robert Altman, but Rudolph has never sought the glitz and gloss of Hollywood, content to remain on the fringe. Zoom in on his filmography, however, and think of the romantic little picture that starred Timothy Hutton, *Made in Heaven*, and the Jennifer Jason Leigh vehicle *Mrs Parker and the Vicious Circle*, both vintage Rudolph. Anyone who hasn't yet discovered a Rudolph will be pleasantly surprised to discover a world of complex relationships and strong characterisation.

Ratataplan   1979

Directed by: Maurizio Nichetti
Written by: Maurizio Nichetti
Cast: Maurizio Nichetti (Colombo), Lidia Biondi (Pregnant Woman), Roland Topor (Boss), Angela Finocchiaro (Unpretty Girl).

Story: An unemployed engineer named Colombo (Nichetti) searches for work and... love.

Nichetti's directional debut is this hilarious silent comedy, with Maurizio just using facial expressions, body language, gestures and music to convey the message. The film was made for 100 million lire and grossed six billion lire worldwide after its success at the Venice Film Festival.

RARITY RATING: 4/5
Available in Italy with English subtitles but has been re-edited for the international market.

Maurizio Nichetti: An inventive genius whose brand of comedy is a mixture of Chaplin and Woody Allen. He garnered the attention of critics and audiences alike with his film *The Icicle Thief*, which was a monochrome homage to De Sica's *Bicycle Thieves*, and follows the storyline of a director who is invited on a TV programme to discuss his movie before a screening. The show is interrupted by commercials and the characters move from their world into the other. The director then has to step in to sort out the mess.

This was a preview of Nichetti's creativity and entering his world is like visiting an emporium of magical metamorphosis. In 1991, he directed *Volere Volare*, with Guido Manuli, in which he played a sound-effects man who finds himself changing into a cartoon figure when he falls in love with a woman. It was vintage Nichetti and epitomised his work ethic of fusing fantasy and reality.

THE 1980s

A guy named Indiana was being chased by a boulder, an alien creature wanted to go home, a blow-up doll was flying a plane, Johnnie was chopping through a door, Sarandon washed with lemons, Martin was getting help from Marlowe and Spade, swordsmen were levitating through trees, Mia Farrow found herself in the film that she was watching, dancing was becoming dirty, and a classroom of kids were standing on their desks. But not all things were healthy, and one cinema was threatened with closure.

HealtH   1980

Directed by: Robert Altman
Written by: Robert Altman. Frank Barhydt.
Cast: Carol Burnett (Gloria Burbank), Glenda Jackson (Isabella Garnell), James Garner (Harry Wolff), Lauren Bacall (Esther Brill), Paul Dooley (Dr Gil Gainey).

Story: A satirical look at the health and fitness craze and set entirely at a health-food convention at a Florida hotel. The title is an acronym: Happiness, Energy And Longevity Through Health, and it opens with a presidential campaign for the organisation. The leading candidates for the post are Esther Brill (Bacall), a senile 83 year old, and a crusty old pessimist, Isabella Gamell (Jackson). Standing as an independent candidate is a Dr Gil Gainey (Dooley). Carol Burnett plays Gloria Burbank, a White House advisor, Henry Gibson is Bobby Hammer, a dirty tricks campaigner, and Alfre Woodard is the hotel manager, Sally Benbow.

Like all Altman films, not only does this send up politics but also film; so unconventional and often uncommercial. But then that's their attraction. There are some very funny scenes, though admittedly time has taken its toll on a number of gags. The hilarious scene in which the hotel manager is interviewed by Dick Cavett transcends its era though. The film was meant for release during the presidential campaign of 1980, but 20th Century Fox decided to withdraw the film for two years.

RARITY RATING: 4/5
Besides airings on cable television, the film is not availble.

Robert Altman: His first feature film *The Delinquents* impressed Hitchcock so much that he invited him to direct some of the Hitchcock Hour TV series. Altman has been impressing and inspiring filmmakers and cinephiles ever since. His films attract the crème de la crème of actors: Tim Robbins, Susan Sarandon, Jack Lemmon, Donald Sutherland, Elliott Gould, Warren Beatty, Julie Christie, Lauren Bacall, Lily Tomlin, Meryl Streep, James Garner, Woody Harrelson. Sound was used naturally in Altman's films and dialogue would often fade away or into incoherence as in reality. He dispensed with the conventional screenplay and allowed his actors to create their own dialogue and mannerisms in a way that made the viewer feel as if they were eavesdropping on a piece of life. Altman likened his filmmaking method to jazz: 'You're not planning any of this that you film. You're capturing.'

The Player is a perfect example of Altman's improvised imagery with people walking in and out of shots or performing in the background of a scene. The film centres on a studio executive, Griffin Mill (Robbins), who starts to receive death threats from a screenwriter whose work he has rejected. It is a brilliant piece of cinema that one never tires of watching. Like all his films, Altman produced clarity out of chaos. He died in 2007, aged 81.

Andrina   1981

Directed by: Bill Forsyth
Written by: Bill Forsyth. George Mackay Brown (story).
Cast: Cyril Cusack. Wendy Jane Morgan. Sandra Voe.

Story: There is little known about *Andrina* except that it was originally shown on BBC television and has since not been seen. Any film that is missing from the Forsyth filmography is sadly lamented. What is even harder to understand is that the film belongs to the BBC and they could release it tomorrow. Even the leading actress Wendy Jane Morgan has disappeared from film and television, *Andrina* being her only film. I for one would dearly love to see it again.

RARITY RATING: 5/5
Watch BBC television listings. No DVD or VHS available.

Bill Forsyth: There are no bad guys in Forsyth's films, only warm and quirky ones. Forsyth made only nine films but each in its own way provided a memorable experience for the discerning cinemagoer. There was *Gregory's Girl*, a magical story about a young lad who suddenly discovers an interest in girls that supersedes his passion for football. *Comfort and Joy* delights with its whimsical telling of an ice-cream war waged between vendors, with a disc jockey, Alan Bird, played perfectly by Bill Paterson, endeavouring to act as mediator. *Local Hero* showed the transformation of an American executive who is sent to Scotland to buy a small fishing village and instead falls in love with its local customs and way of life; even the brownish, dark beer. *Housekeeping* is an enchanting yet strange tale of an aunt who keeps house for two young orphans. Here we witness the eccentricities of the aunt, played by Christine Lahti, preferring to sit for hours in the dark, or going for long walks, or hoarding old newspapers and tin cans. His films are beautiful observations of characters that you rarely meet in life yet somehow wished that you had.

Where is Parsifal?   1983

Directed by: Henri Helman
Written by: Berta Dominguez
Cast: Tony Curtis (Parsifal), Orson Welles (Klingsor), Berta Dominguez (Elba).

Story: A thinly disguised biopic of the Salkinds, Alexander and Berta, and written by the latter as a vehicle for her to star in using the pseudonym Berta Dominguez. Alex's part is played by Tony Curtis and Christopher Chaplin plays Berta's real son, Ilya. In the story, Parsifal, the inventor of skywriting, lives in a huge house with many strange guests and is trying to sell some of his inventions to raise money. Nothing is made very clear.

Apparently, the film was never made for public exhibition and never released in cinemas. It reflects the bizarre world and egos of the Salkinds and has become a cult favourite because of its rarity and because it was the last screen appearance of Welles who played Klingsor, a cousin of Berta's.

RARITY RATING: 5/5
Unshown, and as DVD sales often depend on theatrical release and promotion, likely to remain that way.

Nothing Left To Do But Cry   1985

Directed by: Roberto Benigni
Written by: Roberto Benigni. Giuseppe Bertolucci.
Cast: Massimo Troisi (Mario), Roberto Benigni (Saverio), Iris Peynado (Astriaha).

Story: A teacher and a janitor, Saverio (Benigni) and Mario (Troisi) inadvertently travel back in time to 1492 taking with them all of their unresolved disputes, particularly those concerning Saverio's sister.

They are continually making fools of themselves by not realising the time period they are in, such as when they try to hitch a lift back to the future. The twosome meets some great historical figures such as Leonardo da Vinci, who they mistake for an idiot. They also encounter Columbus and the heretic Savonarola on his way to be burnt at the stake. Saverio falls in and out of love with women, while Mario finds women love him because he is generous and kind.

Considered to be one of the finest comedies ever to have come out of Italy, it remains unknown to many both at home and abroad. The reason given for its neglect and thus its rarity is one of translation, because it used Neapolitan and Tuscan dialects for its leading actors. It was considered that few outside of Italy would understand it despite subtitles. However, both Troisi and Benigni are masters of mime and body language and the loss of this gem seems to be totally wasteful.

RARITY RATING: 5/5
Only an overdue homage to one or both of its stars might encourage its release to DVD.

Roberto Benigni: Like Nichetti, Benigni is an inventive genius and mimic. *Life is Beautiful*, his most successful film to date, won him two Oscars for Best Actor and for Best Foreign Film. It is a modern masterpiece that tells the story of an imaginative waiter, gifted with a sense of humour, who must use those same characteristic traits when he and his wife and son are imprisoned in a concentration camp during World War Two, in order to survive. To protect his young son, he tells him that everything that is happening to them is a game. Besides the obvious Chaplinesque moments of comedy there is a distinct texture to the film that is poignantly visualised in tones of vibrant colours in the early Mediterranean sequences contrasted with scenes drained of colour once in the setting of the concentration camp.

The Tiger and the Snow attempted to reprise the same formula as *Life is Beautiful* by moving the storyline to the Middle East. Benigni is a poet in Iraq during the Gulf War who tries to save the woman he loves when she is injured. This film, like *Nothing Left To Do But Cry*, seems to have become a neglected classic, but at least its survival has been assured by its DVD release.

THE 1990s

Lester Burnham was fantasising about his daughter's girlfriend, Hannibal Lecter was contemplating washing down liver and some fava beans with a nice chianti, a kid didn't want to be left alone, there was a déjà vu happening on top of the Empire State, brontosauruses were running around in a park, Muriel was sending out invitations, Mr White was losing a lot of red, a brother and sister got trapped in a television series, and a gentle giant was frying in a chair. Unfortunately some films were dying because of lack of distribution.

The Golden Sword   1990

Directed by: Gennadi Shumsky. Stanislav Sokolov.
Written by: Alexander Alexandrov. Gennadi Shumsky. Stanislav Sokolov.
Cast: Lena Loginova (Choura)

Story: Choura (Loginova) feels rejected by her childhood friend Igor, who now seems to live in a different world from her. She likes nature while he loves cars. By accident Choura discovers an underground world inhabited by living puppets and dolls. One of them is a handsome flying prince who possesses a golden sword with magic powers. The prince falls in love with Choura and decides that he must enter and confront the modern world with his golden sword. But what will happen to him?

This is a beautiful and charming fairy tale with all the qualities of an Alice in Wonderland and one of the finest children's films ever to come out of Russia. The puppets are simply marvellous and the story quite enchanting.

RARITY RATING: 5/5
Unforgettable if seen, unforgivable if not.

The Voyage of Captain Fracassa   1990

Directed by: Ettore Scola
Written by: Vincenzo Cerami (story). Theophile Gautier (novel).
Cast: Vincent Perez (Baron of Sigognac), Emmanuelle Beart (Isabella), Massimo Troisi (Pulcinella), Ornella Muti (Serafina).

Story: A fantasy tale about a young royal, Baron of Sigognac (Perez), whose desire for material wealth leads him to true love by meeting Isabella (Beart) and joining a troupe of travelling actors. Gone is the insecure man, replaced by a confident and charismatic performer. The Baron is aided by a Sancho Panza type of clown named Pulcinella (Troisi).

This is a wonderful comedy that contains pearls of wisdom. Beautifully photographed and acted by an excellent cast. Troisi is totally memorable as Pulcinella.

RARITY RATING: 5/5
Hard to believe that a film that has been described as a masterpiece by the few that have seen it, has disappeared.

A Woman Champion   1990

Directed by: Elisabeta Bostan
Written by: Rock Demers, Vasilica Istrate.
Cast: Izabela Moldovan (Corina), Mircea Diaconu (Mitran), Carmen Galin (Lili).

Story: Obviously inspired by the Romanian success of Nadia Come-nechi, this film traces the hard work and dedication it takes to be a gymnastic champion. We see the teachers are also hard taskmasters but the overriding message is that you can do anything that you want to do if you believe that you can.

Wonderfully inspiring, particularly to children.

RARITY RATING: 4/5
DVD release is long overdue.

The Angel of Pennsylvania Avenue   1996

Directed by: Robert Ellis Miller
Written by: Rider McDowell. Michael De Guzman.
Cast: Robert Urich (Angus Feagan), Diana Scarwid (Mrs Annie Feagan), Tegan Moss (Bernice Feagan), Britney Irvin (Lilly Feagan).

Story: Based on the true story of the Feagans – Bernice, Lilly and Jack, played by Tegan Moss, Britney Irvin and Alexander Pollock – who trav-elled to Washington and the White House to get their father pardoned from prison. The action by the children successfully allowed President Hoover (Thomas Peacocke) to release Angus Feagan (Urich) from his custodial sentence.

A good attempt but somewhat dated now. Urich was particularly fine.

RARITY RATING: 4/5
Probably not commercial enough to warrant a DVD issue.

A Corner of Paradise   1997

Directed by: Peter Ringgaard
Written by: John Bernstein. Bob Foss.

Cast: Samuel Froeler (Nils von Ekelow), Trine Pallesan (Anna), John Savage (Padre Louis), Penelope Cruz (Dona Helena).

Story: A brave man's attempt to save the rain forests of Costa Rica. Nils von Ekelow (Froeler) journeys from Stockholm to Costa Rica after his dismissal from the Swedish army and the rejection of his master's thesis by his academic committee. Once in South America, Nils begins his thorough research and discovers that the rain forest and its Indian inhabitants are being eradicated by land barons using Dioxin, commonly known as Agent Orange and used many years later in the Vietnam war. Among his distractions are his girlfriend and one of the baron's daughters. His eventual success with his mission led to a national forest being named in his honour, but unfortunately he didn't live to see it.

Beautifully photographed and savouring each moment, *A Corner of Paradise* was unfairly criticised for its slow pace. The film is also noted for giving Penelope Cruz her first English-speaking part. Good support is given to Froeler, one of Sweden's top actors.

RARITY RATING: 4/5
A Corner of Paradise would appeal to environmentalists, if they were ever given a chance to see it.

PLEASE RELEASE ME

A young, aspiring journalist tries to gatecrash a concert and falls for Penny Lane, a thirtysomething sings all by herself, JM Barrie meets his Peter Pan, a neurotic guy is concerned that his girlfriend thinks they don't communicate any more but she doesn't want to talk about it, and a night custodian at the Museum of Cinema watches Buster Keaton films. Alas, some films were being watched at maybe their one and only screening.

Honolulu Baby   2001

Directed by: Maurizio Nichetti
Written by: Giovanna Carrassi. Richard Clement Haber.
Cast: Maurizio Nichetti (Alberto Colombo), Maria de Medeiros (Margherita), Jean Rochefort (Cri Cri), Paulina Galvez (Marilda).

Story: Reprising his role of Colombo in *Ratataplan*, Nichetti moves the story forward to see his character fearing for his job at a multinational company. The Italian employees are forced to speak English, while his wife Margherita (de Medeiros) encourages them to speak English at home. When the company sends Colombo to a South American backwater town from which no one has ever returned, he thinks it could be the end for him. Instead he finds a paradise of beautiful women starved of men. The only man he encounters is Cri Cri (Rochefort) who admits that 300 women are too much for even a Frenchman to handle.

A blend of four languages – Italian, Spanish, French and pidgin English – it was shot entirely on digital.

RARITY RATING: 5/5
Multi-lingual, it has proved difficult for subtitling.

The Old Man Who Read Love Stories   2001

Directed by: Rolf de Heer
Written by: Claude Cohen (French dialogue). Luis Sepulveda (novel).
Cast: Richard Dreyfuss (Antonio Bolivar), Timothy Spall (Luis Agalla).

Story: Antonio Bolivar (Dreyfuss) reads his first romantic novel while hunting a jaguar in the Amazon jungle. The animal he is forced to confront symbolises his own past and the love he has for the beast and the dilemma he now faces of killing it.

A trademark quirky story, offering the unexpected in unusual surroundings, featuring extraordinarily good performances.

RARITY RATING: 3/5
Was available on DVD at Amazon but has since been discontinued.

I Am   2005

Directed by: Dorota Kedzierzawska
Written by: Dorota Kedzierzawska
Cast: Piotr Jagielski (Kundel), Agnieszka Nagorzycka (Kuleczka).

Story: An 11-year-old boy with the sobriquet of Mongrel escapes from a children's home and takes refuge in a derelict shed. A 9-year-old girl from a wealthy family, Kuleczka, which means Marble in English, befriends the boy. She has a drink problem and, because they share issues, a rapport develops between them that leads to love. Mongrel roams the town finding scrap metal that he sells to an old man.

Based on a real-life story of a homeless boy, this film is beautifully poignant due to incredible performances by the child actors.

RARITY RATING: 4/5
An arthouse video company will surely release this film once the public appreciate the work of Kedzierzawska.

Dorota Kedzierzawska: Daughter of a Polish film director, Jadwiga Kedzierzawska, Kedzierzawska has stamped her indelible mark on the ten films that she has directed, from her first *Agnieszka* in 1980 to her latest *Pora umierac* in 2006. She has a particularly insightful way of using and portraying children in her films: *The Crows* was about a young girl, called Crow because she mimics the bird, who kidnaps a younger girl and mothers her and gives her the affection that she wished she received from her own mother; *I Am* showed a similar understanding.

The Courage to Love 2005

Directed by: Claude Lelouch
Written by: Claude Lelouch
Cast: Mathilde Seigner (Clementine/Anne), Malwenn Le Besco (Shaa), Massimo Ranieri (Massimo), Michel Leeb (Michel Gorkini).

Story: This was originally going to be part of Lelouch's planned *Humankind* trilogy, but the first two parts, *The Parisians* and *Men and Women*, were omitted after poor press response and only *The Courage To Love* remains. Lelouch still keeps a lone print of *Men and Women*, but *The Courage To Love* is the sole version available for export, pared down to 103 minutes. There are still story threads from the second version that have crossed over and been kept for this cut. The film is filled with the Lelouch trademark of extreme close ups and beautifully photographed images.

Though little publicity has been given to this final print, there is undoubtedly an air of anticipation that it will get a wider audience both theatrically and in the home entertainment market.

RARITY RATING: 4/5
Definitely one for Criterion.

Claude Lelouch: 'Filmmaking is like spermatozoa. Only one in a million makes it.' Lelouch has had a continued love affair with film that has seen him make almost 50 films, in which only one can be said to have 'made it'; and *A Man and a Woman* was undoubtedly a consummate hit. Despite its success, its sequel, *A Man and a Woman: 20 Years Later*, was unable to capitalise on the fond memory of the original. Lelouch is a brilliant filmmaker, however, who makes films that visually, if not always cerebrally, caress the heart. His contribution to the recent homage film to Cannes, *To Each His Cinema*, was the 3-minute visual vignette *Cinema de Boulevard*. A man sings in hushed tones the song *Cheek to Cheek* to his loved one while sitting in a cinema as Fred Astaire sings the same song to Ginger Rogers on the screen. It's this type of movie magic that separates the true cinema artist from a million others.

The Unknown   2006

Directed by: Giuseppe Tornatore
Written by: Giuseppe Tornatore. Massimo De Rita.

Story: Irena is a young Ukrainian woman living in an unidentified Italian city and she has brought with her a past of violence and humiliation. She manages to get employment as a house servant to a wealthy couple with a little girl. In a short time she becomes fond of the family, particularly the little girl. But then suddenly someone appears from her past bringing new horrors.

Quite a departure for Tornatore who is remembered for his romantic hymn to the cinema, *Cinema Paradiso*; *The Unknown* is an outright psychological thriller with all the requisite nail-biting moments of that genre.

RARITY RATING: 1/5
Optimistically we can expect this to be released on DVD but there are no guarantees and a lot will depend on how the film performs at the box office.

Giuseppe Tornatore: With only ten films in the can, Tornatore is not the most prolific of directors but then, with the international acclaim of *Cinema Paradiso*, he can afford the luxury of long siestas. *Malena* is the only film to come close to *Paradiso*'s success. The eponymous heroine, played by Monica Bellucci, awakens a sleepy village with her voluptuousness when she walks down the street, and particularly the desire of one young boy who worships her. But who is she really? Whether his films are hits or misses, they are always compulsive viewing.

ACKNOWLEDGEMENTS

The author would like to thank the following organisations and reference material, which were consulted during the writing of this book.

DVDs

John Cassavetes Five Films – The Criterion Collection.
Chacun son Cinema – Studio Canal.
Z Channel: A Magnificent Obsession – Hart Sharp Video.

BOOKS

Peter Bogdanovich (2005) *Who The Hell's In It?* Faber and Faber: London.
Paul Duncan (2004) *Alfred Hitchcock*. Pocket Essentials: Harpenden, Hertfordshire.
Paul Duncan (2004) *Film Noir*. Pocket Essentials: Harpenden, Hertfordshire.
Martin Fitzgerald (2002) *Orson Welles*. Pocket Essentials: Harpenden, Hertfordshire.
Ben Gazzara (2004) *In The Moment*. Carroll & Graf Publishers: New York.
Louis Giannetti (2002) *Understanding Movies* – Ninth Edition. Prentice-Hall International (UK) Limited.
Pauline Kael (1991) *5001 Nights At The Movies*. Owl Books. Henry Holt and Company: New York.

Lillian Ross & Helen Ross (1962) *The Player*. Simon & Schuster: New York.

Time Out Film Guides. Penguin: London.

Quinlan's Illustrated Directory of Film Stars. B.T. Batsford: London.

ORGANISATIONS

The British Film Institute.

WEBSITES

www.5minutestolive.com
www.imdb.com

INDEX

kamera
BOOKS

ESSENTIAL READING FOR ANYONE INTERESTED
IN FILM AND POPULAR CULTURE

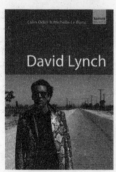

Tackling a wide range of subjects from prominent directors, popular genres and current trends through to cult films, national cinemas and film concepts and theories. Kamera Books come complete with complementary DVDs packed with additional material, including feature films, shorts, documentaries and interviews.

www.kamerabooks.com